MARTIN LUTHER

BASIC LUTHER

- The 95 Theses
- Address to the Nobility
- Concerning Christian Liberty
- A Small Catechism

Templegate Publishers

©Templegate Publishers 1984

Printed in the United States of America

Templegate Publishers
302 E. Adams Street
P.O. Box 5152
Springfield, IL 62705

ISBN 0-87243-131-2

Table of Contents

INTRODUCTORY NOTE

MARTIN LUTHER, *the leader of the Protestant Reformation, was born at Eisleben, Prussian Saxony, November 10, 1483. He studied jurisprudence at the University of Erfurt, where he later lectured on physics and ethics. In 1505 he entered the Augustinian monastery at Erfurt; two years later was ordained priest; and in 1508 became professor of philosophy at the University of Wittenberg.*

The starting-point of Luther's career as a reformer was his proclamation at Wittenberg of the Ninety-five Theses on October 31, 1517. These formed a passionate statement of the true nature of penitence, and a protest against the sale of indulgences. In issuing the Theses, Luther expected the support of his ecclesiastical superiors; and it was only after three years of controversy, during which he refused a summons to Rome, that he proceeded to publish those works that brought about his expulsion from the Church.

The year 1520 saw the publication of the three great documents which laid down the fundamental principles of the Reformation. In the "Address to the Christian Nobility of the German Nation," Luther attacked the corruptions of the Church and the abuses of its authority, and asserted the right of the layman to spiritual independence. In "Concerning Christian Liberty," he expounded the doctrine of justification by faith, and gave a complete presentation of his theological position. In the "Babylonish Captivity of the Church," he criticized the sacramental system, and set up the Scriptures as the supreme authority in religion.

In the midst of this activity came his formal excommunication, and his renunciation of allegiance to the Pope. He was proscribed by the Emperor Charles V and taken into the protection of prison in the Wartburg by the friendly Elector of Saxony, where he translated the New Testament. The complete translation of the Bible, issued in 1534, marks the establishment of the modern literary language of Germany.

The rest of Luther's life was occupied with a vast amount of literary and controversial activity. He died at Eisleben, February 18, 1546.

INTRODUCTORY LETTER

To the most Reverend Father in Christ and most illustrious Lord, Albert, Archbishop and Primate of the Churches of Magdeburg and Mentz, Marquis of Brandenburg, etc., his lord and pastor in Christ, most gracious and worthy of all fear and reverence—

JESUS

The grace of God be with you, and whatsoever it is and can do.

Spare me, most reverend Father in Christ, most illustrious Prince, if I, the very dregs of humanity, have dared to think of addressing a letter to the eminence of your sublimity. The Lord Jesus is my witness that, in the consciousness of my own pettiness and baseness, I have long put off the doing of that which I have now hardened my forehead to perform, moved thereto most especially by the sense of that faithful duty which I feel that I owe to your most reverend Fatherhood in Christ. May your Highness then in the meanwhile deign to cast your eyes upon one grain of dust, and, in your pontifical clemency, to understand my prayer.

Papal indulgences are being carried about, under your most distinguished authority, for the building of St. Peter's. In respect of these, I do not so much accuse the extravagant sayings of the preachers, which I have not heard, but I grieve at the very false ideas which the people conceive from them, and which are spread abroad in common talk on every side—namely, that unhappy souls believe that, if they buy letters of indulgences, they are sure of their salvation; also, that, as soon as they have thrown their contribution into the chest, souls forthwith fly out of purgatory; and furthermore, that so great is the grace thus conferred, that there is no sin so great—even, as they say, if, by an impossibility, any one had violated the Mother of God—but that it may be pardoned; and again, that by these indulgences a man is freed from all punishment and guilt.

O gracious God! it is thus that the souls committed to your care, most excellent Father, are being taught unto their death, and a most severe account, which you will have to render for all of them, is growing and increasing. Hence I have not been able to keep silence any longer on this subject, for by no function of a bishop's office can a man become sure of salvation, since he does not even become sure through the grace of God infused into him, but the Apostle bids us to be ever working out our salvation in fear and trembling. (Phil. ii. 12.) Even the righteous man—says Peter—shall scarcely be saved. (I Peter iv. 18.) In fine, so narrow is the way which leads unto life, that the Lord, speaking by the prophets Amos and Zachariah, calls those who are to be saved brands snatched from the burning, and our Lord everywhere declares the difficulty of salvation.

Why, then, by these false stories and promises of pardon, do the preachers of them make the people to feel secure and without fear? since indulgences confer absolutely no good on souls as regards salvation or holiness, but only take away the outward penalty which was wont of old to be canonically imposed.

Lastly, works of piety and charity are infinitely better than indulgences, and yet they do not preach these with such display or so much zeal; nay, they keep silence about them for the sake of preaching pardons. And yet it is the first and sole duty of all bishops, that the people should learn the Gospel and Christian charity: for Christ nowhere commands that indulgences should be preached. What a dreadful thing it is then, what peril to a bishop, if, while the Gospel is passed over in silence, he permits nothing but the noisy outcry of indulgences to be spread among his people, and bestows more care on these than on the Gospel! Will not Christ say to them: "Straining at a gnat, and swallowing a camel"?

Besides all this, most reverend Father in the Lord, in that instruction to the commissaries which has been put forth under the name of your most reverend Fatherhood it is stated—doubtless without the knowledge and consent of your most reverend

Fatherhood—that one of the principal graces conveyed by indulgences is that inestimable gift of God, by which man is reconciled to God, and all the pains of purgatory are done away with; and further, that contrition is not necessary for those who thus redeem souls or buy confessional licences.

But what can I do, excellent Primate and most illustrious Prince, save to entreat your reverend Fatherhood, through the Lord Jesus Christ, to deign to turn on us the eye of fatherly care, and to suppress that advertisement altogether and impose on the preachers of pardons another form of preaching, lest perchance some one should at length arise who will put forth writings in confutation of them and of their advertisements, to the deepest reproach of your most illustrious Highness. It is intensely abhorrent to me that this should be done, and yet I fear that it will happen, unless the evil be speedily remedied.

This faithful discharge of my humble duty I entreat that your most illustrious Grace will deign to receive in a princely and bishoplike spirit—that is, with all clemency—even as I offer it with a most faithful heart, and one most devoted to your most reverend Fatherhood, since I too am part of your flock. May the Lord Jesus keep your most reverend Fatherhood for ever and ever. Amen.

From Wittenberg, on the eve of All Saints, in the year 1517.

If it so please your most reverend Fatherhood, you may look at these Disputations, that you may perceive how dubious a matter is that opinion about indulgences, which they disseminate as if it were most certain.

To your most reverend Fatherhood,
MARTIN LUTHER.

THE NINETY-FIVE THESES

DISPUTATION OF DR. MARTIN LUTHER CONCERNING PENITENCE AND INDULGENCES

IN the desire and with the purpose of elucidating the truth, a disputation will be held on the underwritten propositions at Wittenberg, under the presidency of the Reverend Father Martin Luther, Monk of the Order of St. Augustine, Master of Arts and of Sacred Theology, and ordinary Reader of the same in that place. He therefore asks those who cannot be present and discuss the subject with us orally, to do so by letter in their absence. In the name of our Lord Jesus Christ. Amen.

1. Our Lord and Master Jesus Christ, in saying "Repent ye,"[1] etc., intended that the whole life of believers should be penitence.

2. This word cannot be understood of sacramental penance, that is, of the confession and satisfaction which are performed under the ministry of priests.

3. It does not, however, refer solely to inward penitence; nay such inward penitence is naught, unless it outwardly produces various mortifications of the flesh.

4. The penalty[2] thus continues as long as the hatred of self—that is, true inward penitence—continues: namely, till our entrance into the kingdom of heaven.

5. The Pope has neither the will nor the power to remit any penalties, except those which he has imposed by his own authority, or by that of the canons.

6. The Pope has no power to remit any guilt, except by declaring and warranting it to have been remitted by God; or at most by remitting cases reserved for himself; in which cases, if his power were despised, guilt would certainly remain.

---

[1] In the Latin, from the Vulgate, *"agite pœnitentiam,"* sometimes translated "Do penance." The effect of the following theses depends to some extent on the double meaning of *"pœnitentia"*—penitence and penance.

[2] I. e. *"Pœna,"* the connection between *"pœna"* and *"pœnitentia"* being again suggestive.

7. God never remits any man's guilt, without at the same time subjecting him, humbled in all things, to the authority of his representative the priest.

8. The penitential canons are imposed only on the living, and no burden ought to be imposed on the dying, according to them.

9. Hence the Holy Spirit acting in the Pope does well for us, in that, in his decrees, he always makes exception of the article of death and of necessity.

10. Those priests act wrongly and unlearnedly, who, in the case of the dying, reserve the canonical penances for purgatory.

11. Those tares about changing of the canonical penalty into the penalty of purgatory seem surely to have been sown while the bishops were asleep.

12. Formerly the canonical penalties were imposed not after, but before absolution, as tests of true contrition.

13. The dying pay all penalties by death, and are already dead to the canon laws, and are by right relieved from them.

14. The imperfect soundness or charity of a dying person necessarily brings with it great fear; and the less it is, the greater the fear it brings.

15. This fear and horror is sufficient by itself, to say nothing of other things, to constitute the pains of purgatory, since it is very near to the horror of despair.

16. Hell, purgatory, and heaven appear to differ as despair, almost despair, and peace of mind differ.

17. With souls in purgatory it seems that it must needs be that, as horror diminishes, so charity increases.

18. Nor does it seem to be proved by any reasoning or any scriptures, that they are outside of the state of merit or of the increase of charity.

19. Nor does this appear to be proved, that they are sure and confident of their own blessedness, at least all of them, though we may be very sure of it.

20. Therefore the Pope, when he speaks of the plenary remission of all penalties, does not mean simply of all, but only of those imposed by himself.

21. Thus those preachers of indulgences are in error who say that, by the indulgences of the Pope, a man is loosed and saved from all punishment.

22. For in fact he remits to souls in purgatory no penalty which they would have had to pay in this life according to the canons.

23. If any entire remission of all penalties can be granted to any one, it is certain that it is granted to none but the most perfect—that is, to very few.

24. Hence the greater part of the people must needs be deceived by this indiscriminate and high-sounding promise of release from penalties.

25. Such power as the Pope has over purgatory in general, such has every bishop in his own diocese, and every curate in his own parish, in particular.

26. The Pope acts most rightly in granting remission to souls, not by the power of the keys (which is of no avail in this case), but by the way of suffrage.

27. They preach mad, who say that the soul flies out of purgatory as soon as the money thrown into the chest rattles.

28. It is certain that, when the money rattles in the chest, avarice and gain may be increased, but the suffrage of the Church depends on the will of God alone.

29. Who knows whether all the souls in purgatory desire to be redeemed from it, according to the story told of Saints Severinus and Paschal?

30. No man is sure of the reality of his own contrition, much less of the attainment of plenary remission.

31. Rare as is a true penitent, so rare is one who truly buys indulgences—that is to say, most rare.

32. Those who believe that, through letters of pardon, they are made sure of their own salvation, will be eternally damned along with their teachers.

33. We must especially beware of those who say that these pardons from the Pope are that inestimable gift of God by which man is reconciled to God.

34. For the grace conveyed by these pardons has respect only to the penalties of sacramental satisfaction, which are of human appointment.

35. They preach no Christian doctrine, who teach that contrition is not necessary for those who buy souls out of purgatory or buy confessional licences.

36. Every Christian who feels true compunction has of right plenary remission of pain and guilt, even without letters of pardon.

37. Every true Christian, whether living or dead, has a share in all the benefits of Christ and of the Church given him by God, even without letters of pardon.

38. The remission, however, imparted by the Pope is by no means to be despised, since it is, as I have said, a declaration of the Divine remission.

39. It is a most difficult thing, even for the most learned theologians, to exalt at the same time in the eyes of the people the ample effect of pardons and the necessity of true contrition.

40. True contrition seeks and loves punishment; while the ampleness of pardons relaxes it, and causes men to hate it, or at least gives occasion for them to do so.

41. Apostolical pardons ought to be proclaimed with caution, lest the people should falsely suppose that they are placed before other good works of charity.

42. Christians should be taught that it is not the mind of the Pope that the buying of pardons is to be in any way compared to works of mercy.

43. Christians should be taught that he who gives to a poor man, or lends to a needy man, does better than if he bought pardons.

44. Because, by a work of charity, charity increases and the man becomes better; while, by means of pardons, he does not become better, but only freer from punishment.

45. Christians should be taught that he who sees any one in need, and passing him by, gives money for pardons, is not purchasing for himself the indulgences of the Pope, but the anger of God.

46. Christians should be taught that, unless they have superfluous wealth, they are bound to keep what is necessary for the use of their own households, and by no means to lavish it on pardons.

47. Christians should be taught that, while they are free to buy pardons, they are not commanded to do so.

48. Christians should be taught that the Pope, in granting pardons, has both more need and more desire that devout prayer should be made for him, than that money should be readily paid.

49. Christians should be taught that the Pope's pardons are useful, if they do not put their trust in them; but most hurtful, if through them they lose the fear of God.

50. Christians should be taught that, if the Pope were acquainted with the exactions of the preachers of pardons, he would prefer that the Basilica of St. Peter should be burnt to ashes, than that it should be built up with the skin, flesh and bones of his sheep.

51. Christians should be taught that, as it would be the duty, so it would be the wish of the Pope, even to sell, if necessary, the Basilica of St. Peter, and to give of his own money to very many of those from whom the preachers of pardons extract money.

52. Vain is the hope of salvation through letters of pardon, even if a commissary—nay, the Pope himself—were to pledge his own soul for them.

53. They are enemies of Christ and of the Pope who, in order that pardons may be preached, condemn the word of God to utter silence in other churches.

54. Wrong is done to the word of God when, in the same sermon, an equal or longer time is spent on pardons than on it.

55. The mind of the Pope necessarily is, that if pardons, which are a very small matter, are celebrated with single bells, single processions, and single ceremonies, the Gospel, which is a very great matter, should be preached with a hundred bells, a hundred processions, and a hundred ceremonies.

56. The treasures of the Church, whence the Pope grants in-

dulgences, are neither sufficiently named nor known among the people of Christ.

57. It is clear that they are at least not temporal treasures, for these are not so readily lavished, but only accumulated, by many of the preachers.

58. Nor are they the merits of Christ and of the saints, for these, independently of the Pope, are always working grace to the inner man, and the cross, death, and hell to the outer man.

59. St. Lawrence said that the treasures of the Church are the poor of the Church, but he spoke according to the use of the word in his time.

60. We are not speaking rashly when we say that the keys of the Church, bestowed through the merits of Christ, are that treasure.

61. For it is clear that the power of the Pope is alone sufficient for the remission of penalties and of reserved cases.

62. The true treasure of the Church is the Holy Gospel of the glory and grace of God.

63. This treasure, however, is deservedly most hateful, because it makes the first to be last.

64. While the treasure of indulgences is deservedly most acceptable, because it makes the last to be first.

65. Hence the treasures of the gospel are nets, wherewith of old they fished for the men of riches.

66. The treasures of indulgences are nets, wherewith they now fish for the riches of men.

67. Those indulgences, which the preachers loudly proclaim to be the greatest graces, are seen to be truly such as regards the promotion of gain.

68. Yet they are in reality in no degree to be compared to the grace of God and the piety of the cross.

69. Bishops and curates are bound to receive the commissaries of apostolical pardons with all reverence.

70. But they are still more bound to see to it with all their eyes, and take heed with all their ears, that these men do not preach their own dreams in place of the Pope's commission.

71. He who speaks against the truth of apostolical pardons, let him be anathema and accursed.

72. But he, on the other hand, who exerts himself against the wantonness and licence of speech of the preachers of pardons, let him be blessed.

73. As the Pope justly thunders against those who use any kind of contrivance to the injury of the traffic in pardons.

74. Much more is it his intention to thunder against those who, under the pretext of pardons, use contrivances to the injury of holy charity and of truth.

75. To think that Papal pardons have such power that they could absolve a man even if—by an impossibility—he had violated the Mother of God, is madness.

76. We affirm, on the contrary, that Papal pardons cannot take away even the least of venal sins, as regards its guilt.

77. The saying that, even if St. Peter were now Pope, he could grant no greater graces, is blasphemy against St. Peter and the Pope.

78. We affirm, on the contrary, that both he and any other Pope have greater graces to grant—namely, the Gospel, powers, gifts of healing, etc. (I Cor. xii. 9.)

79. To say that the cross set up among the insignia of the Papal arms is of equal power with the cross of Christ, is blasphemy.

80. Those bishops, curates, and theologians who allow such discourses to have currency among the people, will have to render an account.

81. This licence in the preaching of pardons makes it no easy thing, even for learned men, to protect the reverence due to the Pope against the calumnies, or, at all events, the keen questionings of the laity.

82. As for instance:—Why does not the Pope empty purgatory for the sake of most holy charity and of the supreme necessity of souls—this being the most just of all reasons—if he redeems an infinite number of souls for the sake of that most fatal thing, money, to be spent on building a basilica—this being a very slight reason?

83. Again: why do funeral masses and anniversary masses for the deceased continue, and why does not the Pope return, or permit the withdrawal of the funds bequeathed for this purpose, since it is a wrong to pray for those who are already redeemed?

84. Again: what is this new kindness of God and the Pope, in that, for money's sake, they permit an impious man and an enemy of God to redeem a pious soul which loves God, and yet do not redeem that same pious and beloved soul, out of free charity, on account of its own need?

85. Again: why is it that the penitential canons, long since abrogated and dead in themselves in very fact and not only by usage, are yet still redeemed with money, through the granting of indulgences, as if they were full of life?

86. Again: why does not the Pope, whose riches are at this day more ample than those of the wealthiest of the wealthy, build the one Basilica of St. Peter with his own money, rather than with that of poor believers?

87. Again: what does the Pope remit or impart to those who, through perfect contrition, have a right to plenary remission and participation?

88. Again: what greater good would the Church receive if the Pope, instead of once, as he does now, were to bestow these remissions and participations a hundred times a day on any one of the faithful?

89. Since it is the salvation of souls, rather than money, that the Pope seeks by his pardons, why does he suspend the letters and pardons granted long ago, since they are equally efficacious?

90. To repress these scruples and arguments of the laity by force alone, and not to solve them by giving reasons, is to expose the Church and the Pope to the ridicule of their enemies, and to make Christian men unhappy.

91. If, then, pardons were preached according to the spirit and mind of the Pope, all these questions would be resolved with ease—nay, would not exist.

92. Away, then, with all those prophets who say to the people of Christ, "Peace, peace," and there is no peace!

93. Blessed be all those prophets who say to the people of Christ, "The cross, the cross," and there is no cross!

94. Christians should be exhorted to strive to follow Christ their Head through pains, deaths, and hells.

95. And thus trust to enter heaven through many tribulations, rather than in the security of peace.

PROTESTATION

I, Martin Luther, Doctor, of the Order of Monks at Wittenberg, desire to testify publicly that certain propositions against pontifical indulgences, as they call them, have been put forth by me. Now although, up to the present time, neither this most celebrated and renowned school of ours, nor any civil or ecclesiastical power has condemned me, yet there are, as I hear, some men of headlong and audacious spirit, who dare to pronounce me a heretic, as though the matter had been thoroughly looked into and studied. But on my part, as I have often done before, so now too, I implore all men, by the faith of Christ, either to point out to me a better way, if such a way has been divinely revealed to any, or at least to submit their opinion to the judgment of God and of the Church. For I am neither so rash as to wish that my sole opinion should be preferred to that of all other men, nor so senseless as to be willing that the word of God should be made to give place to fables, devised by human reason.

DEDICATORY LETTER

To the respected and worthy Nicolaus von Amsdorff, Licentiate in the Holy Scriptures and Canon of Wittenberg,[1] *my particular and affectionate friend.   Dr. Martinus Luther.*

The grace and peace of God be with you, respected, worthy Sir, and dear friend!

The time for silence is gone, and the time to speak has come, as we read in Ecclesiastes (iii. 7). I have, in conformity with our resolve, put together some few points concerning the *reformation of the Christian estate,* with the intent of placing the same before the *Christian nobility of the German nation,* in case it may please God to help His Church by means of the laity, inasmuch as the clergy, whom this task rather befitted, have become quite careless. I send all this to your worship, to judge and to amend where needed. I am well aware that I shall not escape the reproach of taking far too much upon me in presuming, insignificant and forsaken as I am, to address such high estates on such weighty and great subjects, as if there were no one in the world but Dr. Luther to have a care for Christianity and to give advice to such wise people.

Let who will blame me, I shall not offer any excuse. Perhaps I still owe God and the world another folly. This debt I have now resolved honestly to discharge, as well as may be, and to be Court fool for once in my life; if I fail, I shall at any rate gain this advantage: that no one need buy me a fool's cap or shave my poll. But it remains to be seen which shall hang the bells on the other. I must fulfil the proverb, "When anything is to be done in the world, a monk must be in it, were it only as a painted figure." I suppose it has often happened that a fool has spoken wisely, and wise men have often done foolishly, as St.

[1]Nicolaus von Amsdorff (1483-1565) was a colleague of Luther at the university of Wittenberg, and one of his most zealous fellow-workers in the cause of the Reformation.

14

Paul says, "If any man among you seemeth to be wise in this world, let him become a fool, that he may be wise (I Cor. iii. 18).

Now, inasmuch as I am not only a fool, but also a sworn doctor of the Holy Scriptures, I am glad that I have an opportunity of fulfilling my oath, just in this fool's way. I beg you to excuse me to the moderately wise, for I know not how to deserve the favour and grace of the supremely wise, which I have so often sought with much labour, but now for the future shall neither have nor regard.

God help us to seek not our glory, but His alone. Amen.

Wittenberg, in the monastry of St. Augustine, on the eve of St. John the Baptist in the year 1520.

JESUS

INTRODUCTION

To his most Serene and Mighty Imperial Majesty and to the Christian Nobility of the German Nation.

Dr. Martinus Luther.

THE grace and might of God be with you, Most Serene Majesty, most gracious, well-beloved gentlemen!

It is not out of mere arrogance and perversity that I, an individual poor man, have taken upon me to address your lordships. The distress and misery that oppress all the Christian estates, more especially in Germany, have led not only myself, but every one else, to cry aloud and to ask for help, and have now forced me too to cry out and to ask if God would give His Spirit to any one to reach a hand to His wretched people. Councils have often put forward some remedy, but it has adroitly been frustrated, and the evils have become worse, through the cunning of certain men. Their malice and wickedness I will now, by the help of God, expose, so that, being known, they may henceforth cease to be so obstructive and injurious. God has given us a young and noble sovereign,[2] and by this has roused great hopes in many hearts; now it is right that we too should do what we can, and make good use of time and grace.

The first thing that we must do is to consider the matter with great earnestness, and, whatever we attempt, not to trust in our own strength and wisdom alone, even if the power of all the world were ours; for God will not endure that a good work should be begun trusting to our own strength and wisdom. He destroys it; it is all useless, as we read in Psalm xxxiii., "There is no king saved by the multitude of a host; a mighty man is not delivered by much strength." And I fear it is for that reason that those beloved princes the Emperors Frederick, the First and the

---

[2]Charles V. was at that time not quite twenty years of age.

17

Second, and many other German emperors were, in former times, so piteously spurned and oppressed by the popes, though they were feared by all the world. Perchance they trusted rather in their own strength than in God; therefore they could not but fall; and how would the sanguinary tyrant Julius II. have risen so high in our own days but that, I fear, France, Germany, and Venice trusted to themselves? The children of Benjamin slew forty-two thousand Israelites, for this reason: that these trusted to their own strength (Judges xx., etc.).

That such a thing may not happen to us and to our noble Emperor Charles, we must remember that in this matter we wrestle not against flesh and blood, but against the rulers of the darkness of this world (Eph. vi. 12), who may fill the world with war and bloodshed, but cannot themselves be overcome thereby. We must renounce all confidence in our natural strength, and take the matter in hand with humble trust in God; we must seek God's help with earnest prayer, and have nothing before our eyes but the misery and wretchedness of Christendom, irrespective of what punishment the wicked may deserve. If we do not act thus, we may begin the game with great pomp; but when we are well in it, the spirits of evil will make such confusion that the whole world will be immersed in blood, and yet nothing be done. Therefore let us act in the fear of God and prudently. The greater the might of the foe, the greater is the misfortune, if we do not act in the fear of God and with humility. If popes and Romanists have hitherto, with the devil's help, thrown kings into confusion, they may still do so, if we attempt things with our own strength and skill, without God's help.

THE THREE WALLS OF THE ROMANISTS

The Romanists have, with great adroitness, drawn three walls round themselves, with which they have hitherto protected themselves, so that no one could reform them, whereby all Christendom has fallen terribly.

Firstly, if pressed by the temporal power, they have affirmed and maintained that the temporal power has no jurisdiction over them, but, on the contrary, that the spiritual power is above the temporal.

Secondly, if it were proposed to admonish them with the Scriptures, they objected that no one may interpret the Scriptures but the Pope.

Thirdly, if they are threatened with a council, they pretend that no one may call a council but the Pope.

Thus they have secretly stolen our three rods, so that they may be unpunished, and intrenched themselves behind these three walls, to act with all the wickedness and malice, which we now witness. And whenever they have been compelled to call a council, they have made it of no avail by binding the princes beforehand with an oath to leave them as they were, and to give moreover to the Pope full power over the procedure of the council, so that it is all one whether we have many councils or no councils, in addition to which they deceive us with false pretences and tricks. So grievously do they tremble for their skin before a true, free council; and thus they have overawed kings and princes, that these believe they would be offending God, if they were not to obey them in all such knavish, deceitful artifices.

Now may God help us, and give us one of those trumpets that overthrew the walls of Jericho, so that we may blow down these walls of straw and paper, and that we may set free our Christian rods for the chastisement of sin, and expose the craft and deceit of the devil, so that we may amend ourselves by punishment and again obtain God's favour.

(a) THE FIRST WALL

That the Temporal Power has no Jurisdiction over the Spiritualty

Let us, in the first place, attack the first wall.

It has been devised that the Pope, bishops, priests, and monks are called the *spiritual estate*, princes, lords, artificers, and peasants are the *temporal estate.* This is an artful lie and hypocritical device, but let no one be made afraid by it, and that for this reason: that all Christians are truly of the spiritual estate, and there is no difference among them, save of office alone. As St. Paul says (I Cor. xii.), we are all one body, though each member does its own work, to serve the others. This is because we have one baptism, one Gospel, one faith, and are all Christians alike; for baptism, Gospel, and faith, these alone make spiritual and Christian people.

As for the unction by a pope or a bishop, tonsure, ordination, consecration, and clothes differing from those of laymen—all this may make a hypocrite or an anointed puppet, but never a Christian or a spiritual man. Thus we are all consecrated as priests by baptism, as St. Peter says: "Ye are a royal priesthood, a holy nation" (I Peter ii. 9); and in the book of Revelations: "and hast made us unto our God (by Thy blood) kings and priests" (Rev. v. 10). For, if we had not a higher consecration in us than pope or bishop can give, no priest could ever be made by the consecration of pope or bishop, nor could he say the mass, or preach, or absolve. Therefore the bishop's consecration is just as if in the name of the whole congregation he took one person out of the community, each member of which has equal power, and commanded him to exercise this power for the rest; in the same way as if ten brothers, co-heirs as king's sons, were to choose one from among them to rule over their inheritance, they would all of them still remain kings and have equal power, although one is ordered to govern.

And to put the matter even more plainly, if a little company of pious Christian laymen were taken prisoners and carried away to a desert, and had not among them a priest consecrated by a bishop, and were there to agree to elect one of them, born in wedlock or not, and were to order him to baptise, to celebrate the mass, to absolve, and to preach, this man would as truly be a priest, as if all the bishops and all the popes had consecrated him. That is why in cases of necessity every man can baptise and absolve, which would not be possible if we were not all priests.

This great grace and virtue of baptism and of the Christian estate they have quite destroyed and made us forget by their ecclesiastical law. In this way the Christians used to choose their bishops and priests out of the community; these being afterwards confirmed by other bishops, without the pomp that now prevails. So was it that St. Augustine, Ambrose, Cyprian, were bishops.

Since, then, the temporal power is baptised as we are, and has the same faith and Gospel, we must allow it to be priest and bishop, and account its office an office that is proper and useful to the Christian community. For whatever issues from baptism may boast that it has been consecrated priest, bishop, and pope, although it does not beseem every one to exercise these offices. For, since we are all priests alike, no man may put himself forward or take upon himself, without our consent and election, to do that which we have all alike power to do. For, if a thing is common to all, no man may take it to himself without the wish and command of the community. And if it should happen that a man were appointed to one of these offices and deposed for abuses, he would be just what he was before. Therefore a priest should be nothing in Christendom but a functionary; as long as he holds his office, he has precedence of others; if he is deprived of it, he is a peasant or a citizen like the rest. Therefore a priest is verily no longer a priest after deposition. But now they have invented *characteres indelebiles,*[3] and pretend that a priest after deprivation still differs from a simple layman. They even imagine that a priest can never be anything but a priest—that is, that he can never become a layman. All this is nothing but mere talk and ordinance of human invention.

It follows, then, that between laymen and priests, princes and bishops, or, as they call it, between spiritual and temporal persons, the only real difference is one of office and function, and

[3]In accordance with a doctrine of the Roman Catholic Church, the act of ordination impresses upon the priest an indelible character; so that he immutably retains the sacred dignity of priesthood.

not of estate; for they are all of the same spiritual estate, true priests, bishops, and popes, though their functions are not the same—just as among priests and monks every man has not the same functions. And this, as I said above, St. Paul says (Rom. xii.; I Cor. xii.), and St. Peter (I Peter ii.): "We, being many, are one body in Christ, and severally members one of another." Christ's body is not double or twofold, one temporal, the other spiritual. He is one Head, and He has one body.

We see, then, that just as those that we call spiritual, or priests, bishops, or popes, do not differ from other Christians in any other or higher degree but in that they are to be concerned with the word of God and the sacraments—that being their work and office—in the same way the temporal authorities hold the sword and the rod in their hands to punish the wicked and to protect the good. A cobbler, a smith, a peasant, every man, has the office and function of his calling, and yet all alike are consecrated priests and bishops, and every man should by his office or function be useful and beneficial to the rest, so that various kinds of work may all be united for the furtherance of body and soul, just as the members of the body all serve one another.

Now see what a Christian doctrine is this: that the temporal authority is not above the clergy, and may not punish it. This is as if one were to say the hand may not help, though the eye is in grievous suffering. Is it not unnatural, not to say unchristian, that one member may not help another, or guard it against harm? Nay, the nobler the member, the more the rest are bound to help it. Therefore I say, Forasmuch as the temporal power has been ordained by God for the punishment of the bad and the protection of the good, therefore we must let it do its duty throughout the whole Christian body, without respect of persons, whether it strikes popes, bishops, priests, monks, nuns, or whoever it may be. If it were sufficient reason for fettering the temporal power that it is inferior among the offices of Christianity to the offices of priest or confessor, or to the spiritual estate—if this were so, then we ought to restrain tailors, cobblers, masons, carpenters, cooks, cellarmen, peasants, and all secular workmen, from providing the Pope or bishops, priests and monks, with shoes, clothes, houses or victuals, or from paying them tithes. But if these laymen are allowed to do their work without restraint, what do the Romanist scribes mean by their laws? They mean that they withdraw themselves from the operation of temporal Christian power, simply in order that they may be free to do evil, and thus fulfil what St. Peter said: "There shall be false teachers among you, . . . and in covetousness shall they with feigned words make merchandise of you" (2 Peter ii. 1, etc.).

Therefore the temporal Christian power must exercise its office without let or hindrance, without considering whom it may strike, whether pope, or bishop, or priest: whoever is guilty, let him suffer for it.

Whatever the ecclesiastical law has said in opposition to this is merely the invention of Romanist arrogance. For this is what St. Paul says to all Christians: "Let every soul" (I presume including the popes) "be subject unto the higher powers; for they bear not the sword in vain: they serve the Lord therewith, for vengeance on evildoers and for praise to them that do well" (Rom. xiii. 1-4). Also St. Peter: "Submit yourselves to every ordinance of man for the Lord's sake, . . . for so is the will of God" (I Peter ii. 13, 15). He has also foretold that men would come who should despise government (2 Peter ii.), as has come to pass through ecclesiastical law.

Now, I imagine, the first paper wall is overthrown, inasmuch as the temporal power has become a member of the Christian body; although its work relates to the body, yet does it belong to the spiritual estate. Therefore, it must do its duty without let or hindrance upon all members of the whole body, to punish or urge, as guilt may deserve, or need may require, without respect of pope, bishops, or priests, let them threaten or excommunicate as they will. That is why a guilty priest is deprived of his priesthood before being given over to the secular arm; whereas this would not be right, if the secular sword had not authority over him already by Divine ordinance.

It is, indeed, past bearing that the spiritual law should esteem so highly the liberty, life, and property of the clergy, as if laymen were not as good spiritual Christians, or not equally members of the Church. Why should your body, life, goods, and honour be free, and not mine, seeing that we are equal as Christians, and have received alike baptism, faith, spirit, and all things? If a priest is killed, the country is laid under an interdict[4]: why not also if a peasant is killed? Whence comes this great difference among equal Christians? Simply from human laws and inventions.

It can have been no good spirit, either, that devised these evasions and made sin to go unpunished. For if, as Christ and the Apostles bid us, it is our duty to oppose the evil one and all his works and words, and to drive him away as well as may be, how then should we remain quiet and be silent when the Pope and his followers are guilty of devilish works and words? Are we for the sake of men to allow the commandments and the truth of God to be defeated, which at our baptism we vowed to support with body and soul? Truly we should have to answer for all souls that would thus be abandoned and led astray.

Therefore it must have been the arch-devil himself who said, as we read in the ecclesiastical law, If the Pope were so perniciously wicked, as to be dragging souls in crowds to the devil, yet he could not be deposed. This is the accursed and devilish foundation on which they build at Rome, and think that the whole world is to be allowed to go to the devil rather than they should be opposed in their knavery. If a man were to escape punishment simply because he is above the rest, then no Christian might punish another, since Christ has commanded each of us to esteem himself the lowest and the humblest (Matt. xviii. 4; Luke ix. 48).

Where there is sin, there remains no avoiding the punishment,

---

[4] By the *Interdict,* or general excommunication, whole countries, districts, or towns, or their respective rulers, were deprived of all the spiritual benefits of the Church, such as Divine service, the administering of the sacraments, etc.

as St. Gregory says, We are all equal, but guilt makes one subject to another. Now let us see how they deal with Christendom. They arrogate to themselves immunities without any warrant from the Scriptures, out of their own wickedness, whereas God and the Apostles made them subject to the secular sword; so that we must fear that it is the work of antichrist, or a sign of his near approach.

(b) THE SECOND WALL

That no one may interpret the Scriptures but the Pope

The second wall is even more tottering and weak: that they alone pretend to be considered masters of the Scriptures; although they learn nothing of them all their life. They assume authority, and juggle before us with impudent words, saying that the Pope cannot err in matters of faith, whether he be evil or good, albeit they cannot prove it by a single letter. That is why the canon law contains so many heretical and unchristian, nay unnatural, laws; but of these we need not speak now. For whereas they imagine the Holy Ghost never leaves them, however unlearned and wicked they may be, they grow bold enough to decree whatever they like. But were this true, where were the need and use of the Holy Scriptures? Let us burn them, and content ourselves with the unlearned gentlemen at Rome, in whom the Holy Ghost dwells, who, however, can dwell in pious souls only. If I had not read it, I could never have believed that the devil should have put forth such follies at Rome and find a following.

But not to fight them with our own words, we will quote the Scriptures. St. Paul says, "If anything be revealed to another that sitteth by, let the first hold his peace" (I Cor. xiv. 30). What would be the use of this commandment, if we were to believe him alone that teaches or has the highest seat? Christ Himself says, "And they shall be all taught of God." (St. John vi. 45). Thus it may come to pass that the Pope and his followers are wicked and not true Christians, and not being taught by God, have no true understanding, whereas a common man may have true understanding. Why should we then not follow him? Has not the Pope often erred? Who could help Christianity, in case the Pope errs, if we do not rather believe another who has the Scriptures for him?

Therefore it is a wickedly devised fable—and they cannot quote a single letter to confirm it—that it is for the Pope alone to interpret the Scriptures or to confirm the interpretation of them. They have assumed the authority of their own selves. And though they say that this authority was given to St. Peter when the keys were given to him, it is plain enough that the keys were not given to St. Peter alone, but to the whole community. Besides, the keys were not ordained for doctrine or authority, but for sin, to bind or loose; and what they claim besides this from the keys is mere invention. But what Christ said to St. Peter: "I have prayed for thee that thy faith fail not" (St. Luke xxii. 32), cannot relate to the Pope, inasmuch as the greater part of the Popes have been without faith, as they are themselves forced to acknowledge; nor did Christ pray for Peter alone, but for all the Apostles and all Christians, as He says, "Neither pray I for these alone, but for them also which shall believe on Me through their word" (St. John xvii.). Is not this plain enough?

Only consider the matter. They must needs acknowledge that there are pious Christians among us that have the true faith, spirit, understanding, word, and mind of Christ: why then should we reject their word and understanding, and follow a pope who has neither understanding nor spirit? Surely this were to deny our whole faith and the Christian Church. Moreover, if the article of our faith is right, "I believe in the holy Christian Church," the Pope cannot alone be right; else we must say, "I believe in the Pope of Rome," and reduce the Christian Church to one man, which is a devilish and damnable heresy. Besides that, we are all priests, as I have said, and have all one faith, one Gospel, one Sacrament; how then should we not have the power of discerning and judging what is right or wrong in matters of faith? What becomes of St. Paul's words, "But he that is spiritual judgeth all things, yet he himself is judged of no man" (I Cor. ii. 15), and also, "we having the same spirit of faith"? (2 Cor. iv. 13). Why then should we not perceive as well as an unbelieving pope what agrees or disagrees with our faith?

By these and many other texts we should gain courage and freedom, and should not let the spirit of liberty (as St. Paul has it) be frightened away by the inventions of the popes; we should boldly judge what they do and what they leave undone by our own believing understanding of the Scriptures, and force them to follow the better understanding, and not their own. Did not Abraham in old days have to obey his Sarah, who was in stricter bondage to him than we are to any one on earth? Thus, too, Balaam's ass was wiser than the prophet. If God spoke by an ass against a prophet, why should He not speak by a pious man against the Pope? Besides, St. Paul withstood St. Peter as being in error (Gal. ii.). Therefore it behoves every Christian to aid the faith by understanding and defending it and by condemning all errors.

(c) THE THIRD WALL

That no one may call a council but the Pope

The third wall falls of itself, as soon as the first two have fallen; for if the Pope acts contrary to the Scriptures, we are bound to stand by the Scriptures, to punish and to constrain him, according to Christ's commandment, "Moreover, if thy brother shall trespass against thee, go and tell him his fault between thee and him alone; if he shall hear thee, thou hast gained thy brother. But if he will not hear thee, then take with thee one or two more, that in the mouth of two or three witnesses every word may be established. And if he shall neglect to hear them, tell it unto the Church; but if he neglect to hear the Church, let him be unto thee as a heathen man and a publican" (St. Matt. xviii. 15-17). Here each member is commanded to take care for the other; much more then should we do this, if it is a ruling member of the community that does evil, which by its evil-doing causes great harm and offence to the others. If then I am to accuse him before the Church, I must collect the Church together. Moreover, they can show nothing in the Scriptures giving the Pope sole power to call and confirm councils; they have nothing but their own laws; but these hold good only so long as they are not injurious to Christianity and the laws of God. Therefore, if the Pope deserves punishment, these laws cease to bind us, since Christendom would suffer, if he were not punished by a council. Thus we read (Acts xv.) that the council of the Apostles was not called by St. Peter, but by all the Apostles and the elders. But if the right to call it had lain with St. Peter alone, it would not have been a Christian council, but a heretical *conciliabulum*. Moreover, the most celebrated council of all—that of Nicæa—was neither called nor confirmed by the Bishop of Rome, but by the Emperor Constantine; and after him many other emperors have done the same, and yet the councils called by them were accounted most Christian. But if the Pope alone had the power, they must all have been heretical. Moreover, if I consider the councils that the Pope has called, I do not find that they produced any notable results.

Therefore when need requires, and the Pope is a cause of offence to Christendom, in these cases whoever can best do so, as a faithful member of the whole body, must do what he can to procure a true free council. This no one can do so well as the temporal authorities, especially since they are fellow-Christians, fellow-priests, sharing one spirit and one power in all things, and since they should exercise the office that they have received from God without hindrance, whenever it is necessary and useful that it should be exercised. Would it not be most unnatural, if a fire were to break out in a city, and every one were to keep still and let it burn on and on, whatever might be burnt, simply because they had not the mayor's authority, or because the fire perchance broke out at the mayor's house? Is not every citizen bound in this case to rouse and call in the rest? How much more should this be done in the spiritual city of Christ, if a fire of offence breaks out, either at the Pope's government or wherever it may! The like happens if an enemy attacks a town. The first to rouse up the rest earns glory and thanks. Why then should not he earn glory that descries the coming of our enemies from hell and rouses and summons all Christians?

But as for their boasts of their authority, that no one must oppose it, this is idle talk. No one in Christendom has any authority to do harm, or to forbid others to prevent harm being done. There is no authority in the Church but for reformation. Therefore if the Pope wished to use his power to prevent the calling of a free council, so as to prevent the reformation of the Church, we must not respect him or his power; and if he should begin to excommunicate and fulminate, we must despise this as the doings of a madman, and, trusting in God, excommunicate and repel him as best we may. For this his usurped power is nothing; he does not possess it, and he is at once overthrown by a text from the Scriptures. For St. Paul says to the Corinthians "that God has given us authority for edification, and not for destruction" (2 Cor. x. 8). Who will set this text at nought? It is the power of the devil and of antichrist that prevents what would serve for the reformation of Christendom. Therefore we must not follow it, but oppose it with our body, our goods, and all that we have. And even if a miracle were to happen in favour of the Pope against the temporal power, or if some were to be stricken by a plague, as they sometimes boast has happened, all this is to be held as having been done by the devil in order to injure our faith in God, as was foretold by Christ: "There shall arise false Christs and false prophets, and shall show great signs and wonders, insomuch that, if it were possible, they shall deceive the very elect" (Matt. xxiv. 23); and St. Paul tells the Thessalonians that the coming of antichrist shall be "after the working of Satan with all power and signs and lying wonders" (2 Thess. ii. 9).

Therefore let us hold fast to this: that Christian power can do nothing against Christ, as St. Paul says, "For we can do nothing against Christ, but for Christ'' (2 Cor. xiii. 8). But, if it does anything against Christ, it is the power of antichrist and the devil, even if it rained and hailed wonders and plagues. Wonders and plagues prove nothing, especially in these latter evil days, of which false wonders are foretold in all the Scriptures. Therefore we must hold fast to the words of God with an assured faith; then the devil will soon cease his wonders.

And now I hope the false, lying spectre will be laid with which the Romanists have long terrified and stupefied our consciences. And it will be seen that, like all the rest of us, they are subject to the temporal sword; that they have no authority to interpret the Scriptures by force without skill; and that they have no power to prevent a council, or to pledge it in accordance with their pleasure, or to bind it beforehand, and deprive it of its freedom; and that if they do this, they are verily of the fellowship of antichrist and the devil, and have nothing of Christ but the name.

OF THE MATTERS TO BE CONSIDERED IN THE COUNCILS

Let us now consider the matters which should be treated in the councils, and with which popes, cardinals, bishops, and all learned men should occupy themselves day and night, if they love Christ and His Church. But if they do not do so, the people at large and the temporal powers must do so, without considering the thunders of their excommunications. For an unjust excommunication is better than ten just absolutions, and an unjust absolution is worse than ten just excommunications. Therefore let us rouse ourselves, fellow-Germans, and fear God more than man, that we be not answerable for all the poor souls that are so miserably lost through the wicked, devilish government of the Romanists, and that the dominion of the devil should not grow day by day, if indeed this hellish government can grow any worse, which, for my part, I can neither conceive nor believe.

1. It is a distressing and terrible thing to see that the head of Christendom, who boasts of being the vicar of Christ and the

successor of St. Peter, lives in a worldly pomp that no king or emperor can equal, so that in him that calls himself most holy and most spiritual there is more worldliness than in the world itself. He wears a triple crown, whereas the mightiest kings only wear one crown. If this resembles the poverty of Christ and St. Peter, it is a new sort of resemblance. They prate of its being heretical to object to this; nay, they will not even hear how unchristian and ungodly it is. But I think that if he should have to pray to God with tears, he would have to lay down his crowns; for God will not endure any arrogance. His office should be nothing else than to weep and pray constantly for Christendom and to be an example of all humility.

However this may be, this pomp is a stumbling-block, and the Pope, for the very salvation of his soul, ought to put it off, for St. Paul says, "Abstain from all appearance of evil" (I Thess. v. 21), and again, "Provide things honest in the sight of all men" (2 Cor. viii. 21). A simple mitre would be enough for the pope: wisdom and sanctity should raise him above the rest; the crown of pride he should leave to antichrist, as his predecessors did some hundreds of years ago. They say, He is the ruler of the world. This is false; for Christ, whose vicegerent and vicar he claims to be, said to Pilate, "My kingdom is not of this world" (John xviii. 36). But no vicegerent can have a wider dominion than his Lord, nor is he a vicegerent of Christ in His glory, but of Christ crucified, as St. Paul says, "For I determined not to know anything among you save Jesus Christ, and Him crucified" (2 Cor. ii. 2), and "Let this mind be in you, which was also in Christ Jesus, who made Himself of no reputation, and took upon Himself the form of a servant" (Phil. ii. 5, 7). Again, "We preach Christ crucified" (I Cor. i.). Now they make the Pope a vicegerent of Christ exalted in heaven, and some have let the devil rule them so thoroughly that they have maintained that the Pope is above the angels in heaven and has power over them, which is precisely the true work of the true antichrist.

2. What is the use in Christendom of the people called "cardinals"? I will tell you. In Italy and Germany there are many

rich convents, endowments, fiefs, and benefices, and as the best way of getting these into the hands of Rome, they created cardinals, and gave them the sees, convents, and prelacies, and thus destroyed the service of God. That is why Italy is almost a desert now: the convents are destroyed, the sees consumed, the revenues of the prelacies and of all the churches drawn to Rome; towns are decayed, the country and the people ruined, because there is no more any worship of God or preaching; why? Because the cardinals must have all the wealth. No Turk could have thus desolated Italy and overthrown the worship of God.

Now that Italy is sucked dry, they come to Germany and begin very quietly; but if we look on quietly Germany will soon be brought into the same state as Italy. We have a few cardinals already. What the Romanists mean thereby the drunken Germans[5] are not to see until they have lost everything—bishoprics, convents, benefices, fiefs, even to their last farthing. Antichrist must take the riches of the earth, as it is written (Dan. xi. 8, 39, 43). They begin by taking off the cream of the bishoprics, convents and fiefs; and as they do not dare to destroy everything as they have done in Italy, they employ such holy cunning to join together ten or twenty prelacies, and take such a portion of each annually that the total amounts to a considerable sum. The priory of Würzburg gives one thousand guilders; those of Bamberg, Mayence, Treves, and others also contribute. In this way they collect one thousand or ten thousand guilders, in order that a cardinal may live at Rome in a state like that of a wealthy monarch.

After we have gained this, we will create thirty or forty cardinals on one day, and give one St. Michael's Mount,[6] near Bamberg, and likewise the see of Würzburg, to which belong some rich benefices, until the churches and the cities are

[5] The epithet "drunken was formerly often applied by the Italians to the Germans.

[6] Luther alludes here to the Benedictine convent standing on the *Mönchberg,* or St. Michael's Mount.

desolated; and then we shall say, We are the vicars of Christ, the shepherds of Christ's flocks; those mad, drunken Germans must submit to it. I advise, however, that there be made fewer cardinals, or that the Pope should have to support them out of his own purse. It would be amply sufficient if there were twelve, and if each of them had an annual income of one thousand guilders.

What has brought us Germans to such a pass that we have to suffer this robbery and this destruction of our property by the Pope? If the kingdom of France has resisted it, why do we Germans suffer ourselves to be fooled and deceived? It would be more endurable if they did nothing but rob us of our property; but they destroy the Church and deprive Christ's flock of their good shepherds, and overthrow the service and word of God. Even if there were no cardinals at all, the Church would not perish, for they do nothing for the good of Christendom; all they do is to traffic in and quarrel about prelacies and bishoprics, which any robber could do as well.

3. If we took away ninety-nine parts of the Pope's Court and only left one hundredth, it would still be large enough to answer questions on matters of belief. Now there is such a swarm of vermin at Rome, all called papal, that Babylon itself never saw the like. There are more than three thousand papal secretaries alone; but who shall count the other office-bearers, since there are so many offices that we can scarcely count them, and all waiting for German benefices, as wolves wait for a flock of sheep? I think Germany now pays more to the Pope than it formerly paid the emperors; nay, some think more than three hundred thousand guilders are sent from Germany to Rome every year, for nothing whatever; and in return we are scoffed at and put to shame. Do we still wonder why princes, noblemen, cities, foundations, convents, and people grow poor? We should rather wonder that we have anything left to eat.

Now that we have got well into our game, let us pause a while and show that the Germans are not such fools as not to perceive or understand this Romish trickery. I do not here complain that

God's commandments and Christian justice are despised at Rome; for the state of things in Christendom, especially at Rome, is too bad for us to complain of such high matters. Nor do I even complain that no account is taken of natural or secular justice and reason. The mischief lies still deeper. I complain that they do not observe their own fabricated canon law, though this is in itself rather mere tyranny, avarice, and worldly pomp, than a law. This we shall now show.

Long ago the emperors and princes of Germany allowed the Pope to claim the *annates*[7] from all German benefices; that is, half of the first year's income from every benefice. The object of this concession was that the Pope should collect a fund with all this money to fight against the Turks and infidels, and to protect Christendom, so that the nobility should not have to bear the burden of the struggle alone, and that the priests should also contribute. The popes have made such use of this good simple piety of the Germans that they have taken this money for more than one hundred years, and have now made of it a regular tax and duty; and not only have they accumulated nothing, but they have founded out of it many posts and offices at Rome, which are paid by it yearly, as out of a ground-rent.

Whenever there is any pretence of fighting the Turks, they send out some commission for collecting money, and often send out indulgences under the same pretext of fighting the Turks. They think we Germans will always remain such great and inveterate fools that we will go on giving money to satisfy their unspeakable greed, though we see plainly that neither *annates,* nor absolution money, nor any other—not one farthing—goes against the Turks, but all goes into the bottomless sack. They lie and deceive, form and make covenants with us, of which they do not mean to keep one jot. And all this is done in the holy name of Christ and St. Peter.

This being so, the German nation, the bishops and princes,

---

[7] The duty of paying *annates* to the Pope was established by John XXII. in 1319.

should remember that they are Christians, and should defend
the people, who are committed to their government and protection in temporal and spiritual affairs, from these ravenous
wolves in sheep's clothing that profess to be shepherds and
rulers; and since the *annates* are so shamefully abused, and the
covenants concerning them not carried out, they should not suffer their lands and people to be so piteously and unrighteously
flayed and ruined; but by an imperial or a national law they
should either retain the *annates* in the country, or abolish them
altogether. For since they do not keep to the covenants, they
have no right to the *annates;* therefore bishops and princes are
bound to punish this thievery and robbery, or prevent it, as
justice demands. And herein should they assist and strengthen
the Pope, who is perchance too weak to prevent this scandal by
himself, or, if he wishes to protect or support it, restrain and oppose him as a wolf and tyrant; for he has no authority to do evil
or to protect evil-doers. Even if it were proposed to collect any
such treasure for use against the Turks, we should be wise in
future, and remember that the German nation is more fitted to
take charge of it than the Pope, seeing that the German nation
by itself is able to provide men enough, if the money is forthcom-
ing. This matter of the *annates* is like many other Romish
pretexts.

Moreover, the year has been divided among the Pope and the
ruling bishops and foundations in such wise that the Pope has
taken every other month—six in all—to give away the benefices
that fall in his month; in this way almost all the benefices are
drawn into the hands of Rome, and especially the best livings
and dignities. And those that once fall into the hands of Rome
never come out again, even if they never again fall vacant in the
Pope's month. In this way the foundations come very short of
their rights, and it is a downright robbery, the object of which is
not to give up anything again. Therefore it is now high time to
abolish the Pope's months and to take back again all that has
thereby fallen into the hands of Rome. For all the princes and
nobles should insist that the stolen property shall be returned,

the thieves punished, and that those who abuse their powers shall be deprived of them. If the Pope can make a law on the day after his election by which he takes our benefices and livings to which he has no right, the Emperor Charles should so much the more have a right to issue a law for all Germany on the day after his coronation[8] that in future no livings and benefices are to fall to Rome by virtue of the Pope's month, but that those that have so fallen are to be freed and taken from the Romish robbers. This right he possesses authoritatively by virtue of his temporal sword.

But the see of avarice and robbery at Rome is unwilling to wait for the benefices to fall in one after another by means of the Pope's month; and in order to get them into its insatiable maw as speedily as possible, they have devised the plan of taking livings and benefices in three other ways:—

First, if the incumbent of a free living dies at Rome or on his way thither, his living remains for ever the property of the see of Rome, or I rather should say, the see of robbers, though they will not let us call them robbers, although no one has ever heard or read of such robbery.

Secondly, if a "servant" of the Pope or of one of the cardinals takes a living, or if, having a living, he becomes a "servant" of the Pope or of a cardinal, the living remains with Rome. But who can count the "servants" of the Pope and his cardinals, seeing that if he goes out riding, he is attended by three or four thousand mule-riders, more than any king or emperor? For Christ and St. Peter went on foot, in order that their vicegerents might indulge the better in all manner of pomp. Besides, their avarice has devised and invented this: that in foreign countries also there are many called "papal servants," as at Rome; so that in all parts this single crafty little word "papal servant" brings all benefices to the chair at Rome, and they are kept there for ever. Are not these mischievous, devilish devices? Let us only

[8]At the time when the above was written—June, 1520—the Emperor Charles had been elected, but not yet crowned.

wait a while, Mayence, Magdeburg, and Halberstadt will fall very nicely to Rome, and we shall have to pay dearly for our cardinal.[9] Hereafter all the German bishops will be made cardinals, so that there shall remain nothing to ourselves.

Thirdly, whenever there is any dispute about a benefice; and this is, I think, well-nigh the broadest and commonest road by which benefices are brought to Rome. For where there is no dispute numberless knaves can be found at Rome who are ready to scrape up disputes, and attack livings wherever they like. In this way many a good priest loses his living, or has to buy off the dispute for a time with a sum of money. These benefices, confiscated by right or wrong of dispute, are to be for ever the property of the see of Rome. It would be no wonder, if God were to rain sulphur and fire from heaven and cast Rome down into the pit, as He did formerly to Sodom and Gomorrah. What is the use of a pope in Christendom, if the only use made of his power is to commit these supreme villainies under his protection and assistance? Oh noble princes and sirs, how long will you suffer your lands and your people to be the prey of these ravening wolves?

But these tricks did not suffice, and bishoprics were too slow in falling into the power of Roman avarice. Accordingly our good friend Avarice made the discovery that all bishoprics are abroad in name only, but that their land and soil is at Rome; from this it follows that no bishop may be confirmed until he has bought the "Pall"[10] for a large sum, and has with a terrible oath bound himself a servant of the Pope. That is why no bishop dare

[9] Luther alludes here to the Archbishop Albert of Mayence, who was, besides, Archbishop of Magdeburg and administrator of the bishopric of Halberstadt. In order to be able to defray the expense of the archiepiscopal tax due to Rome, amounting to thirty thousand guilders, he had farmed the sale of the Pope's indulgences, employing the notorious Tetzel as his agent and sharing the profits with the Pope. In 1518 Albert was appointed cardinal. See Ranke, *Deutsche Geschichte,* etc., vol. i., p. 309, etc.

[10] The *Pallium* was since the fourth century the symbol of archiepiscopal power, and had to be redeemed from the Pope by means of a large sum of money and a solemn oath of obedience.

oppose the Pope. This was the object of the oath, and this is how the wealthiest bishoprics have come to debt and ruin. Mayence, I am told, pays twenty thousand guilders. These are true Roman tricks, it seems to me. It is true that they once decreed in the canon law that the *Pall* should be given free, the number of the Pope's servants diminished, disputes made less frequent, that foundations and bishops should enjoy their liberty; but all this brought them no money. They have therefore reversed all this: bishops and foundations have lost all their power; they are mere ciphers, without office, authority, or function; all things are regulated by the chief knaves at Rome, even the offices of sextons and bell-ringers in all churches. All disputes are transferred to Rome; each one does what he will, strong through the Pope's power.

What has happened in this very year? The Bishop of Strasburg, wishing to regulate his see in a proper way and reform it in the matter of Divine service, published some Divine and Christian ordinances for that purpose. But our worthy Pope and the holy chair at Rome overturn altogether this holy and spiritual order on the requisition of the priests. This is what they call being the shepherd of Christ's sheep—supporting priests against their own bishops and protecting their disobedience by Divine decrees. Antichrist, I hope, will not insult God in this open way. There you have the Pope, as you have chosen to have him; and why? Why, because if the Church were to be reformed, there would be danger that it would spread further, so that it might also reach Rome. Therefore it is better to prevent priests from being at one with each other; they should rather, as they have done hitherto, sow discord among kings and princes, and flood the world with Christian blood, lest Christian unity should trouble the holy Roman see with reforms.

So far we have seen what they do with the livings that fall vacant. Now there are not enough vacancies for this delicate greed; therefore it has also taken prudent account of the benefices that are still held by their incumbents, so that they may become vacant, though they are in fact not vacant, and this they effect in many ways.

First, they lie in wait for fat livings or sees which are held by an old or sick man, or even by one afflicted by an imaginary incompetence; him the Roman see gives a *coadjutor,* that is an assistant without his asking or wishing it, for the benefit of the coadjutor, because he is a papal servant, or pays for the office, or has otherwise earned it by some menial sevice rendered to Rome. Thus there is an end of free election on the part of the chapter, or of the right of him who had presented to the living; and all goes to Rome.

Secondly, there is a little word: *commendam,* that is, when the Pope gives a rich and fat convent or church into the charge of a cardinal or any other of his servants, just as I might command you to take charge of one hundred guilders for me. In this way the convent is neither given, nor lent, nor destroyed, nor is its Divine service abolished, but only entrusted to a man's charge, not, however, for him to protect and improve it, but to drive out the one he finds there, to take the property and revenue, and to install some apostate[11] runaway monk, who is paid five or six guilders a year, and sits in the church all day and sells symbols and pictures to the pilgrims; so that neither chanting nor reading in the church goes on there any more. Now if we were to call this the destruction of convents and abolition of Divine service we should be obliged to accuse the Pope of destroying Christianity and abolishing Divine service—for truly he is doing this effectually—but this would be thought harsh language at Rome; therefore it is called a *commendam, or an order to take charge of the convent. In this way the Pope can make commendams* of four or more convents a year, any one of which produces a revenue of more than six thousand guilders. This is the way Divine service is advanced and convents kept up at Rome. This will be introduced into Germany as well.

Thirdly, there are certain benefits that are said to be *incompatible;* that is, they may not be held together according to the

---

[11] Monks who forsook their order without any legal dispensation were called ''apostates.''

canon law, such as two cures, two sees, and the like. Now the Holy See and avarice twists itself out of the canon law by making "glosses," or interpretations, called *Unio*, or *Incorporatio*; that is, several incompatible benefices are incorporated, so that one is a member of the other, and the whole is held to be one benefice: then they are no longer incompatible, and we have got rid of the holy canon law, so that it is no longer binding, except on those who do not buy those *glosses* of the Pope and his *Datarius*.[12] *Unio* is of the same kind: a number of benefices are tied together like a bundle of faggots, and on account of this coupling together they are held to be one benefice. Thus there may be found many a "courtling" at Rome who alone holds twenty-two cures, seven priories, and forty-four prebends, all which is done in virtue of this masterly *gloss,* so as not to be contrary to law. Any one can imagine what cardinals and other prelates may hold. In this way the Germans are to have their purses emptied and their conceit taken out of them.

There is another *gloss* called *Administratio;* that is, that besides his see a man holds an abbey or other high benefice, and possesses all the property of it, without any other title but *administrator.* For at Rome it is enough that words should change, and not deeds, just as if I said, a procuress was to be called a mayoress, yet may remain as good as she is now. Such Romish rule was foretold by St. Peter, when he said, "There shall be false teachers among you, . . . and through covetousness shall they with feigned words make merchandise of you" (2 Peter ii. 1, 3).

This precious Roman avarice has also invented the practice of selling and lending prebends and benefices on condition that the seller or lender has the reversion, so that if the incumbent dies, the benefice falls to him that has sold it, lent it, or abandoned it; in this way they have made benefices heritable property, so that

---

[12] The papal office for the issue and registration of certain documents was called Dataria, from the phrase appended to them, *Datum apud S. Petrum.* The chief of that office, usually a cardinal, bore the title of *Datarius,* or *Pro-datarius.*

none can come to hold them unless the seller sells them to him, or leaves them to him at his death. Then there are many that give a benefice to another in name only, and on condition that he shall not receive a farthing. It is now, too, an old practice for a man to give another a benefice and to receive a certain annual sum, which proceeding was formerly called simony. And there are many other such little things which I cannot recount; and so they deal worse with the benefices than the heathens by the cross dealt with Christ's clothes.

But all this that I have spoken of is old and common at Rome. Their avarice has invented other device, which I hope will be the last and choke it. The Pope has made a noble discovery, called *Pectoralis Reservatio,* that is, "mental reservation"—*et proprius motus,* that is, "and his own will and power." The matter is managed in this way: Suppose a man obtains a benefice at Rome, which is confirmed to him in due form; then comes another, who brings money, or who has done some other service of which the less said the better, and requests the Pope to give him the same benefice: then the Pope will take it from the first and give it him. If you say, that is wrong, the Most Holy Father must then excuse himself, that he may not be openly blamed for having violated justice; and he says "that in his heart and mind he reserved his authority over the said benefice," whilst he never had heard or thought of the same in all his life. Thus he has devised a *gloss* which allows him in his proper person to lie and cheat and fool us all, and all this impudently and in open daylight, and nevertheless he claims to be the head of Christendom, letting the evil spirit rule him with manifest lies.

This wantonness and lying reservation of the popes has brought about an unutterable state of things at Rome. There is a buying and a selling, a changing, blustering and bargaining, cheating and lying, robbing and stealing, debauchery and villainy, and all kinds of contempt of God, that antichrist himself could not rule worse. Venice, Antwerp, Cairo, are nothing to this fair and market at Rome, except that there things are done with some reason and justice, whilst here things are done as the devil himself could wish. And out of this ocean a like virtue overflows all the world. Is it not natural that such people should dread a reformation and a free council, and should rather embroil all kings and princes, than that their unity should bring about a council? Who would like his villainy to be exposed?

Finally, the Pope has built a special house for this fine traffic—that is, the house of the *Datarius* at Rome. Thither all must come that bargain in this way, for prebends and benefices; from him they must buy the *glosses* and obtain the right to practise such prime villainy. In former days it was fairly well at Rome, when justice had to be bought, or could only be put down by money; but now she has become so fastidious that she does not allow any one to commit villainies unless he has first bought the right to do it with great sums. If this is not a house of prostitution, worse than all houses of prostitution that can be conceived, I do not know what houses of prostitution really are.

If you bring money to this house, you can arrive at all that I have mentioned; and more than this, any sort of usury is made legitimate for money; property got by theft or robbery is here made legal. Here vows are annulled; here a monk obtains leave to quit his order; here priests can enter married life for money; here bastards can become legitimate; and dishonour and shame may arrive at high honours; all evil repute and disgrace is knighted and ennobled; here a marriage is suffered that is in a forbidden degree, or has some other defect. Oh, what a trafficking and plundering is there! one would think that the canon laws were only so many money-snares, from which he must free himself who would become a Christian man. Nay, here the devil becomes a saint, and a god besides. What heaven and earth might not do may be done by this house. Their ordinances are called *compositions*—compositions, forsooth! confusions rather.[13] Oh, what a poor treasury is the toll on the Rhine[14] com-

---

[13] Luther uses here the expressions *compositiones* and *confusiones* as a kind of pun.

[14] Tolls were levied at many places along the Rhine.

pared with this holy house!

Let no one think that I say too much. It is all notorious, so that even at Rome they are forced to own that it is more terrible and worse than one can say. I have said and will say nothing of the infernal dregs of private vices. I only speak of well-known public matters, and yet my words do not suffice. Bishops, priests, and especially the doctors of the universities, who are paid to do it, ought to have unanimously written and exclaimed against it. Yea, if you will turn the leaf you will discover the truth.

I have still to give a farewell greeting. These treasures, that would have satisfied three mighty kings, were not enough for this unspeakable greed, and so they have made over and sold their traffic to Fugger[15] at Augsburg, so that the lending and buying and selling sees and benefices, and all this traffic in ecclesiastical property, has in the end come into the right hands, and spiritual and temporal matters have now become one business. Now I should like to know what the most cunning would devise for Romish greed to do that it has not done, except that Fugger might sell or pledge his two trades, that have now become one. I think they must have come to the end of their devices. For what they have stolen and yet steal in all countries by bulls of indulgences, letters of confession, letters of dispensation,[16] and other *confessionalia,* all this I think mere bungling work, and much like playing toss with a devil in hell. Not that they produce little, for a mighty king could support himself by them; but they are as nothing compared to the other streams of revenue mentioned above. I will not now consider what has become of that indulgence money; I shall inquire into this another time, for *Campofiore*[17] and *Belvedere*[18] and some other

---

[15] The commercial house of Fugger was in those days the wealthiest in Europe.

[16] Luther uses the word *Butterbriefe, i. e.,* letters of indulgence allowing the enjoyment of butter, cheese, milk, etc., during Lent. They formed part only of the *confessionalia,* which granted various other indulgences.

[17] A public place at Rome.

[18] Part of the Vatican.

places probably know something about it.

Meanwhile, since this devilish state of things is not only an open robbery, deceit, and tyranny of the gates of hell, but also destroys Christianity body and soul, we are bound to use all our diligence to prevent this misery and destruction of Christendom. If we wish to fight the Turk, let us begin here, where they are worst. If we justly hang thieves and behead robbers, why do we leave the greed of Rome so unpunished, that is the greatest thief and robber that has appeared or can appear on earth, and does all this in the holy name of Christ and St. Peter? Who can suffer this and be silent about it? Almost everything that they possess has been stolen or got by robbery, as we learn from all histories. Why, the Pope never bought those great possessions, so as to be able to raise well-nigh ten hundred thousand ducats from his ec- clesiastical offices, without counting his gold mines described above and his land. He did not inherit it from Christ and St. Peter; no one gave it or lent it him; he has not acquired it by prescription. Tell me, where can he have got it? You can learn from this what their object is when they send out legates to col- lect money to be used against the Turk.

TWENTY-SEVEN ARTICLES RESPECTING THE REFORMATION OF THE CHRISTIAN ESTATE

Now though I am too lowly to submit articles that could serve for the reformation of these fearful evils, I will yet sing out my fool's song, and will show, as well as my wit will allow, what might and should be done by the temporal authorities or by a general council.

1. Princes, nobles, and cities should promptly forbid their sub- jects to pay the *annates* to Rome and should even abolish them altogether. For the Pope has broken the compact, and turned the *annates* into robbery for the harm and shame of the German na- tion; he gives them to his friends; he sells them for large sums of money and founds benefices on them. Therefore he has forfeited his right to them, and deserves punishment. In this way the tem-

poral power should protect the innocent and prevent wrong-doing, as we are taught by St. Paul (Rom. xiii.) and by St. Peter (I Peter ii.) and even by the canon law (16. q. 7. de Filiis). That is why we say to the Pope and his followers, *Tu ora!* "Thou shalt pray"; to the Emperor and his followers, *Tu protege!* "Thou shalt protect"; to the commons, *Tu labora!* "Thou shalt work." Not that each man should not pray, protect, and work; for if a man fulfils his duty, that is prayer, protection, and work; but every man must have his proper task.

2. Since by means of those Romish tricks, *commendams,* coadjutors, reservations, expectations, pope's months, incorporations, unions, Palls, rules of chancellery, and other such knaveries, the Pope takes unlawful possession of all German foundations, to give and to sell them to strangers at Rome, that profit Germany in no way, so that the incumbents are robbed of their rights, and the bishops are made mere ciphers and anointed idols; and thus, besides natural justice and reason, the Pope's own canon law is violated; and things have come to such a pass that prebends and benefices are sold at Rome to vulgar, ignorant asses and knaves, out of sheer greed, while pious learned men have no profit by their merit and skill, whereby the unfortunate German people must needs lack good, learned prelates and suffer ruin—on account of these evils the Christian nobility should rise up against the Pope as a common enemy and destroyer of Christianity, for the sake of the salvation of the poor souls that such tyranny must ruin. They should ordain, order, and decree that henceforth no benefice shall be drawn away to Rome, and that no benefice shall be claimed there in any fashion whatsoever; and after having once got these benefices out of the hands of Romish tyranny, they must be kept from them, and their lawful incumbents must be reinstated in them to administer them as best they may within the German nation. And if a courtling came from Rome, he should receive the strict command to withdraw, or to leap into the Rhine, or whatever river be nearest, and to administer a cold bath to the Interdict, seal and letters and all. Thus those at Rome would learn that we

Germans are not to remain drunken fools forever, but that we, too, are become Christians, and that as such we will no longer suffer this shameful mockery of Christ's holy name, that serves as a cloak for such knavery and destruction of souls, and that we shall respect God and the glory of God more than the power of men.

3. It should be decreed by an imperial law that no episcopal cloak and no confirmation of any appointment shall for the future be obtained from Rome. The order of the most holy and renowned Nicene Council must again be restored, namely that a bishop must be confirmed by the two nearest bishops or by the archbishop. If the Pope cancels the decrees of these and all other councils, what is the good of councils at all? Who has given him the right thus to despise councils and to cancel them? If this is allowed, we had better abolish all bishops, archbishops and primates, and make simple rectors of all of them, so that they would have the Pope alone over them as is indeed the case now; he deprives bishops, archbishops, and primates of all the authority of their office, taking everything to himself, and leaving them only the name and the empty title; more than this, by his exemption he has withdrawn convents, abbots, and prelates from the ordinary authority of the bishops, so that there remains no order in Christendom. The necessary result of this must be, and has been, laxity in punishing and such a liberty to do evil in all the world that I very much fear one might call the Pope "the man of sin" (2 Thess. ii. 3). Who but the Pope is to blame for this absence of all order, of all punishment, of all government, of all discipline, in Christendom? By his own arbitrary power he ties the hands of all his prelates, and takes from them their rods, while all their subjects have their hands unloosed, and obtain licence by gift or purchase.

But, that he have no cause for complaint, as being deprived of his authority, it should be decreed that in cases where the primates and archbishops are unable to settle the matter, or where there is a dispute among them, the matters shall then be submitted to the Pope, but not every little matter, as was done formerly, and was ordered by the most renowned Nicene Council. His Holiness must not be troubled with small matters, that can be settled without his help; so that he may have leisure to devote himself to his prayers and study and to his care of all Christendom, as he professes to do, as indeed the Apostles did, saying, "It is not reason that we should leave the word of God, and serve tables . . . But we will give ourselves continually to prayer, and to the ministry of the word" (Acts vi. 2, 4). But now we see at Rome nothing but contempt of the Gospel and of prayer, and the service of tables, that is the service of the goods of this world, and the government of the Pope agrees with the government of the Apostles as well as Lucifer with Christ, hell with heaven, night with day; and yet he calls himself Christ's vicar and the successor of the Apostles.

4. Let it be decreed that no temporal matter shall be submitted to Rome, but all shall be left to the jurisdiction of the temporal authorities. This is part of their own canon law, though they do not obey it. For this should be the Pope's office: that he, the most learned in the Scriptures and the most holy, not in name only, but in fact, should rule in matters concerning the faith and the holy life of Christians; he should make primates and bishops attend to this, and should work and take thought with them to this end, as St. Paul teaches (I Cor. vi.), severely upbraiding those that occupy themselves with the things of this world. For all countries suffer unbearable damage by this practice of settling such matters at Rome, since it involves great expense; and besides this, the judges at Rome, not knowing the manners, laws, and customs of other countries, frequently pervert the matter according to their own laws and own opinions, thus causing injustice to all parties. Besides this, we should prohibit in all foundations the grievous extortion of the ecclesiastical judges; they should only be allowed to consider matters concerning faith and good morals; but matters concerning money, property, life, and honour should be left to temporal judges. Therefore, the temporal authorities should not permit excommunication or expulsion except in matters of faith and righteous living. It is only

reasonable that spiritual authorities should have power in spiritual matters; spiritual matters, however, are not money or matters relating to the body, but faith and good works.

Still we might allow matters respecting benefices or prebends to be treated before bishops, archbishops, and primates. Therefore when it is necessary to decide quarrels and strifes let the Primate of Germany hold a general consistory, with assessors and chancellors, who would have the control over the *signaturas gratiæ* and *justitiæ*[19] and to whom matters arising in Germany might be submitted by appeal. The officers of such court should be paid out of the *annates,* or in some other way, and should not have to draw their salaries, as at Rome, from chance presents and offerings, whereby they grow accustomed to sell justice and injustice, as they must needs do at Rome, where the Pope gives them no salary, but allows them to fatten themselves on presents; for at Rome no one heeds what is right or what is wrong, but only what is money and what is not money. They might be paid out of the *annates,* or by some other means devised by men of higher understanding and of more experience in these things than I have. I am content with making these suggestions and giving some materials for consideration to those who may be able and willing to help the German nation to become a free people of Christians, after this wretched, heathen, unchristian misrule of the Pope.

5. Henceforth no reservations shall be valid, and no benefices shall be appropriated by Rome, whether the incumbent die there, or there be a dispute, or the incumbent be a servant of the Pope or of a cardinal; and all courtiers shall be strictly prohibited and prevented from causing a ˙dispute about any benefice, so as to cite the pious priests, to trouble them, and to drive them to pay compensation. And if in consequence of this

---

[19] At the time when the above was written the function of the *signatura gratiæ* was to superintend the conferring of grants, concessions, favours, etc., whilst the *signatura justitiæ* embraced the general administration of ecclesiastical matters.

there comes an interdict from Rome, let it be despised, just as if a thief were to excommunicate any man because he would not allow him to steal in peace. Nay, they should be punished most severely for making such a blasphemous use of excommunication and of the name of God, to support their robberies, and for wishing by their false threats to drive us to suffer and approve this blasphemy of God's name and this abuse of Christian authority, and thus to become sharers before God in their wrong-doing, whereas it is our duty before God to punish it, as St. Paul (Rom. i.) upbraids the Romans for not only doing wrong, but allowing wrong to be done. But above all that lying mental reservation (*pectoralis reservatio*) is unbearable, by which Christendom is so openly mocked and insulted, in that its head notoriously deals with lies, and impudently cheats and fools every man for the sake of accursed wealth.

6. The cases reserved[20] (*casus reservati*) should be abolished, by which not only are the people cheated out of much money, but besides many poor consciences are confused and led into error by the ruthless tyrants, to the intolerable harm of their faith in God, especially those foolish and childish cases that are made important by the bull *In Cœna Domini,*[21] and which do not deserve the name of daily sins, not to mention those great cases for which the Pope gives no absolution, such as preventing a pilgrim from going to Rome, furnishing the Turks with arms, or forging the Pope's letters. They only fool us with these gross, mad, and clumsy matters: Sodom and Gomorrah, and all sins that are committed and that can be committed against God's commandments, are not reserved cases; but what God never commanded and they themselves have invented—these must be made reserved cases, solely in order that none may be prevented

[20]"Reserved cases" refer to those great sins for which the Pope or the bishops only could give absolution.

[21]The celebrated papal bull known under the name of *In Cœna Domini,* containing anathemas and excommunications against all those who dissented in any way from the Roman Catholic creed, used until the year 1770 to be read publicly at Rome on Maundy Thursday.

from bringing money to Rome, that they may live in their lust without fear of the Turk, and may keep the world in their bondage by their wicked useless bulls and briefs.

Now all priests ought to know, or rather it should be a public ordinance, that no secret sin constitutes a reserved case, if there be no public accusation; and that every priest has power to absolve from all sin, whatever its name, if it be secret, and that no abbot, bishop, or pope has power to reserve any such case; and, lastly, that if they do this, it is null and void, and they should, moreover, be punished as interfering without authority in God's judgment and confusing and troubling without cause our poor witless consciences. But in respect to any great open sin, directly contrary to God's commandments, there is some reason for a "reserved case"; but there should not be too many, nor should they be reserved arbitrarily without due cause. For God has not ordained tyrants, but shepherds, in His Church, as St. Peter says (I Peter v. 2).

7. The Roman See must abolish the papal offices, and diminish that crowd of crawling vermin at Rome, so that the Pope's servants may be supported out of the Pope's own pocket, and that his court may cease to surpass all royal courts in its pomp and extravagance; seeing that all this pomp has not only been of no service to the Christian faith, but has also kept them from study and prayer, so that they themselves know hardly anything concerning matters of faith, as they proved clumsily enough at the last Roman Council,[22] where, among many childishly trifling matters, they decided "that the soul is immortal," and that a priest is bound to pray once every month on pain of losing his benefice.[23] How are men to rule Christendom and to decide matters of faith who, callous and blinded by their greed, wealth, and worldly pomp, have only just decided that

[22]The council alluded to above was held at Rome from 1512 to 1517.

[23]Luther's objection is not, of course, to the recognition of the immortality of the soul; what he objects to is (1) that it was thought necessary for a council to decree that the soul is immortal, and (2) that this question was put on a level with trivial matters of discipline.

the soul is immortal? It is no slight shame to all Christendom that they should deal thus scandalously with the faith at Rome. If they had less wealth and lived in less pomp, they might be better able to study and pray that they might become able and worthy to treat matters of belief as they were once, when they were content to be bishops, and not kings of kings.

8. The terrible oaths must be abolished which bishops are forced, without any right, to swear to the Pope, by which they are bound like servants, and which are arbitrarily and foolishly decreed in the absurd and shallow chapter *Significasti*.[24] Is it not enough that they oppress us in goods, body, and soul by all their mad laws, by which they have weakened faith and destroyed Christianity; but must they now take possession of the very persons of bishops, with their offices and functions, and also claim the *investiture*[25] which used formerly to be the right of the German emperors, and is still the right of the King in France and other kingdoms? This matter caused many wars and disputes with the emperors until the popes impudently took the power by force, since which time they have retained it, just as if it were only right for the Germans, above all Christians on earth, to be the fools of the Pope and the Holy See, and to do and suffer what no one beside would suffer or do. Seeing then that this is mere arbitrary power, robbery, and a hindrance to the exercise of the bishop's ordinary power, and to the injury of poor souls, therefore it is the duty of the Emperor and his nobles to prevent and punish this tyranny.

9. The Pope should have no power over the Emperor, except to anoint and crown him at the altar, as a bishop crowns a king; nor should that devilish pomp be allowed that the Emperor should kiss the Pope's feet or sit at his feet, or, as it is said, hold his stirrup or the reins of his mule, when he mounts to ride; much less should he pay homage to the Pope, or swear alle-

[24]The above is the title of a chapter in the *Corpus Juris Canonici*.
[25]The right of investiture was the subject of the dispute between Gregory VII. and Henry IV., which led to the Emperor's submission at Canossa.

giance, as is impudently demanded by the popes, as if they had a right to it. The chapter *Solite*,[26] in which the papal authority is exalted above the imperial, is not worth a farthing, and so of all those that depend on it or fear it; for it does nothing but pervert God's holy words from their true meaning, according to their own imaginations, as I have proved in a Latin treatise.

All these excessive, over-presumptuous, and most wicked claims of the Pope are the invention of the devil, with the object of bringing in antichrist in due course and of raising the Pope above God, as indeed many have done and are now doing. It is not meet that the Pope should exalt himself above temporal authority, except in spiritual matters, such as preaching and absolution; in other matters he should be subject to it, according to the teaching of St. Paul (Rom. xiii.) and St. Peter (I Peter iii.), as I have said above. He is not the vicar of Christ in heaven, but only of Christ upon earth. For Christ in heaven, in the form of a ruler, requires no vicar, but there sits, sees, does, knows, and commands all things. But He requires him "in the form of a servant" to represent Him as He walked upon earth, working, preaching, suffering, and dying. But they reverse this: they take from Christ His power as a heavenly Ruler, and give it to the Pope, and allow "the form of a servant" to be entirely forgotten (Phil. ii. 7). He should properly be called the counter-Christ, whom the Scriptures call *antichrist;* for his whole existence, work, and proceedings are directed against Christ, to ruin and destroy the existence and will of Christ.

It is also absurd and puerile for the Pope to boast for such blind, foolish reasons, in his decretal *Pastoralis,* that he is the rightful heir to the empire, if the throne be vacant. Who gave it to him? Did Christ do so when He said, "The kings of the Gentiles exercise lordship over them, but ye shall not do so" (Luke xxii. 25, 26)? Did St. Peter bequeath it to him? It disgusts me that we have to read and teach such impudent, clumsy, foolish lies in the canon law, and, moreover, to take them for Christian

[26] The chapter *Solite* is also contained in the *Corpus Juris Canonici.*

doctrine, while in reality they are mere devilish lies. Of this kind also is the unheard-of lie touching the "donation of Constantine."[27] It must have been a plague sent by God that induced so many wise people to accept such lies, though they are so gross and clumsy that one would think a drunken boor could lie more skilfully. How could preaching, prayer, study, and the care of the poor consist with the government of the empire? These are the true offices of the Pope, which Christ imposed with such insistence that He forbade them to take either coat or scrip (Matt. x. 10), for he that has to govern a single house can hardly perform these duties. Yet the Pope wishes to rule an empire and to remain a pope. This is the invention of the knaves that would fain become lords of the world in the Pope's name, and set up again the old Roman empire, as it was formerly, by means of the Pope and name of Christ, in its former condition.

10. The Pope must withdraw his hand from the dish, and on no pretence assume royal authority over Naples and Sicily. He has no more right to them than I, and yet claims to be the lord—their liege lord. They have been taken by force and robbery, like almost all his other possessions. Therefore the Emperor should grant him no such fief, nor any longer allow him those he has, but direct him instead to his Bibles and Prayer-books, so that he may leave the government of countries and peoples to the temporal power, especially of those that no one has given him. Let him rather preach and pray! The same should be done with Bologna, Imola, Vicenza, Ravenna, and whatever the Pope has taken by force and holds without right in the Ancontine territory, in the Romagna, and other parts of Italy, interfering in their affairs against all the commandments of Christ and St. Paul. For St. Paul says "that he that would be one of the soldiers of heaven must not entangle himself in the

---

[27]In order to legalize the secular power of the Pope, the fiction was invented during the latter part of the eighth century, that Constantine the Great had made over to the popes the dominion over Rome and over the whole of Italy.

affairs of this life'' (2 Tim. ii. 4). Now the Pope should be the
head and the leader of the soldiers of heaven, and yet he engages
more in worldly matters than any king or emperor. He should
be relieved of his worldly cares and allowed to attend to his
duties as a soldier of heaven. Christ also, whose vicar he claims
to be, would have nothing to do with the things of this world,
and even asked one that desired of Him a judgment concerning
his brother, ''Who made Me a judge over you?'' (St. Luke xii.
14). But the Pope interferes in these matters unasked, and concerns himself with all matters, as though he were a god, until he
himself has forgotten what this Christ is whose vicar he professes
to be.

11. The custom of kissing the Pope's feet must cease. It is an
unchristian, or rather an anti-Christian, example that a poor sinful man should suffer his feet to be kissed by one who is a hundred times better than he. If it is done in honour of his power,
why does he not do it to others in honour of their holiness? Compare them together: Christ and the Pope. Christ washed His
disciples' feet and dried them, and the disciples never washed
His. The Pope, pretending to be higher than Christ, inverts this,
and considers it a great favour to let us kiss his feet; whereas, if
any one wished to do so, he ought to do his utmost to prevent
him, as St. Paul and Barnabas would not suffer themselves to be
worshipped as gods by the men at Lystra, saying, ''We also are
men of like passions with you'' (Acts xiv. 14 *seq.*). But our flatterers have brought things to such a pitch that they have set up
an idol for us, until no one regards God with such fear or
honours Him with such marks of reverence as he does the Pope.
This they can suffer, but not that the Pope's glory should be
diminished a single hair's-breadth. Now if they were Christians
and preferred God's honour to their own, the Pope would never
be pleased to have God's honour despised and his own exalted,
nor would he allow any to honour him until he found that God's
honour was again exalted above his own.

It is of a piece with this revolting pride that the Pope is not
satisfied with riding on horseback or in a carriage, but though he

be hale and strong, is carried by men, like an idol in unheard-of pomp. My friend, how does this Lucifer-like pride agree with the example of Christ, who went on foot, as did also all His Apostles? Where has there been a king who has ridden in such worldly pomp as he does, who professes to be the head of all whose duty it is to despise and flee from all worldly pomp—I mean, of all Christians? Not that this need concern us for his own sake, but that we have good reason to fear God's wrath, if we flatter such pride and do not show our discontent. It is enough that the Pope should be so mad and foolish; but it is too much that we should sanction and approve it.

For what Christian heart can be pleased at seeing the Pope when he communicates, sit still like a gracious lord and have the Sacrament handed to him on a golden reed by a cardinal bending on his knees before him? Just as if the Holy Sacrament were not worthy that a pope, a poor miserable sinner, should stand to do honour to his God, although all other Christians, who are much more holy than the Most Holy Father, receive it with all reverence! Could we be surprised if God visited us all with a plague for that we suffer such dishonour to be done to God by our prelates, and approve it, becoming partners of the Pope's damnable pride by our silence or flattery? It is the same when he carries the Sacrament in procession. He must be carried, but the Sacrament stands before him like a cup of wine on a table. In short, at Rome Christ is nothing, the Pope is everything; yet they urge us and threaten us, to make us suffer and approve and honour this anti-Christian scandal, contrary to God and all Christian doctrine. Now may God so help a free council that it may teach the Pope that he too is a man, not above God, as he makes himself out to be.

12. Pilgrimages to Rome must be abolished, or at least no one must be allowed to go from his own wish or his own piety, unless his priest, his town magistrate, or his lord has found that there is sufficient reason for his pilgrimage. This I say, not because pilgrimages are bad in themselves, but because at the present time they lead to mischief; for at Rome a pilgrim sees no

good examples, but only offence. They themselves have made a proverb, "The nearer to Rome, the farther from Christ," and accordingly men bring home contempt of God and of God's commandments. It is said, "The first time one goes to Rome, he goes to seek a rogue; the second time he finds him; the third time he brings him home with him." But now they have become so skilful that they can do their three journeys in one, and they have, in fact, brought home from Rome this saying: "It were better never to have seen or heard of Rome."

And even if this were not so, there is something of more importance to be considered; namely, that simple men are thus led into a false delusion and a wrong understanding of God's commandments. For they think that these pilgrimages are precious and good works; but this is not true. It is but a little good work, often a bad, misleading work, for God has not commanded it. But He has commanded that each man should care for his wife and children and whatever concerns the married state, and should, besides, serve and help his neighbour. Now it often happens that one goes on a pilgrimage to Rome, spends fifty or one hundred guilders more or less, which no one has commanded him, while his wife and children, or those dearest to him, are left at home in want and misery; and yet he thinks, poor foolish man, to atone for this disobedience and contempt of God's commandments by his self-willed pilgrimage, while he is in truth misled by idle curiosity or the wiles of the devil. This the popes have encouraged with their false and foolish invention of *Golden Years*,[28] by which they have incited the people, have torn them away from God's commandments and turned them to their own delusive proceedings, and set up the very thing that they ought to have forbidden. But it brought them money and strengthened

[28] The Jubilees, during which plenary indulgences were granted to those who visited the churches of St. Peter and St. Paul at Rome, were originally celebrated every hundred years and subsequently every twenty-five years. Those who were unable to go to Rome in person could obtain the plenary indulgences by paying the expenses of the journey to Rome into the papal treasury.

their false authority, and therefore it was allowed to continue, though against God's will and the salvation of souls.

That this false, misleading belief on the part of simple Christians may be destroyed, and a true opinion of good works may again be introduced, all pilgrimages should be done away with. For there is no good in them, no commandment, but countless causes of sin and of contempt of God's commandments. These pilgrimages are the reason for there being so many beggars, who commit numberless villainies, learn to beg without need and get accustomed to it. Hence arises a vagabond life, besides other miseries which I cannot dwell on now. If any one wishes to go on a pilgrimage or to make a vow for a pilgrimage, he should first inform his priest or the temporal authorities of the reason, and if it should turn out that he wishes to do it for the sake of good works, let this vow and work be just trampled upon by the priest or the temporal authority as an infernal delusion, and let them tell him to spend his money and the labour a pilgrimage would cost on God's commandments and on a thousandfold better work, namely, on his family and his poor neighbours. But if he does it out of curiosity, to see cities and countries, he may be allowed to do so. If he have vowed it in sickness, let such vows be prohibited, and let God's commandments be insisted upon in contrast to them; so that a man may be content with what he vowed in baptism, namely, to keep God's commandments. Yet for this once he may be suffered, for a quiet conscience' sake, to keep his silly vow. No one is content to walk on the broad high-road of God's commandments; every one makes for himself new roads and new vows, as if he had kept all God's commandments.

13. Now we come to the great crowd that promises much and performs little. Be not angry, my good sirs; I mean well. I have to tell you this bitter and sweet truth: Let no more mendicant monasteries be built! God help us! there are too many as it is. Would to God they were all abolished, or at least made over to two or three orders! It has never done good, it will never do good, to go wandering about over the country. Therefore my advice is that ten, or as many as may be required, be put together

and made into one, which one, sufficiently provided for, need
not beg. Oh! it is of much more importance to consider what is
necessary for the salvation of the common people, than what St.
Francis, or St. Dominic, or St. Augustine,[29] or any other man,
laid down, especially since things have not turned out as they expected. They should also be relieved from preaching and confession, unless specially required to do so by bishops, priests, the
congregation, or other authority. For their preaching and confession has led to nought but mere hatred and envy between priests
and monks, to the great offence and hindrance of the people, so
that it well deserves to be put a stop to, since its place may very
well be dispensed with. It does not look at all improbable that
the Holy Roman See had its own reasons for encouraging all
this crowd of monks: the Pope perhaps feared that priests and
bishops, growing weary of his tyranny, might become too strong
for him, and begin a reformation unendurable to his Holiness.

Besides this, one should also do away with the sections and the
divisions in the same order which, caused for little reason and
kept up for less, oppose each other with unspeakable hatred and
malice, the result being that the Christian faith, which is very
well able to stand without their divisions, is lost on both sides,
and that a true Christian life is sought and judged only by outward rules, works, and practices, from which arise only
hypocrisy and the destruction of souls, as every on can see for
himself. Moreover, the Pope should be forbidden to institute or
to confirm the institution of such new orders; nay, he should be
commanded to abolish several and to lessen their number. For
the faith of Christ, which alone is the important matter, and can
stand without any particular order, incurs no little danger lest
men should be led away by these diverse works and manners
rather to live for such works and practices than to care for faith;
and unless there are wise prelates in the monasteries, who
preach and urge faith rather than the rule of the order, it is

---

[29] The above-mentioned saints were the patrons of the well-known mendicant orders: Franciscans, Dominicans, and Augustines.

inevitable that the order should be injurious and misleading to simple souls, who have regard to works alone.

Now, in our own time all the prelates are dead that had faith and founded orders, just as it was in old days with the children of Israel: when their fathers were dead, that had seen God's works and miracles, their children, out of ignorance of God's work and of faith, soon began to set up idolatry and their own human works. In the same way, alas! these orders, not understanding God's works and faith, grievously labour and torment themselves by their own laws and practices, and yet never arrive at a true understanding of a spiritual and good life, as was foretold by the Apostle, saying of them, "Having a form of godliness, but denying the power thereof, . . . ever learning, and never able to come to the knowledge" of what a true spiritual life is (2 Tim. iii. 2-7). Better to have no convents which are governed by a spiritual prelate, having no understanding of Christian faith to govern them; for such a prelate cannot but rule with injury and harm, and the greater the apparent holiness of his life in external works, the greater the harm.

It would be, I think, necessary, especially in these perilous times, that foundations and convents should again be organised as they were in the time of the Apostles and a long time after, namely when they were all free for every man to remain there as long as he wished. For what were they but Christian schools, in which the Scriptures and Christian life were taught, and where folk were trained to govern and to preach? as we read that St. Agnes went to school, and as we see even now in some nunneries, as at Quedlinburg and other places. Truly all foundations and convents ought to be free in this way: that they may serve God of a free will, and not as slaves. But now they have been bound round with vows and turned into eternal prisons, so that these vows are regarded even more than the vows of baptism. But what fruit has come of this we daily see, hear, read, and learn more and more.

I dare say that this my counsel will be thought very foolish, but I care not for this. I advise what I think best, reject it who will. I know how these vows are kept, especially that of chastity, which is so general in all these convents,[30] and yet was not ordered by Christ, and it is given to comparatively few to be able to keep it, as He says, and St. Paul also (Col. ii. 20). I wish all to be helped, and that Christian souls should not be held in bondage, through customs and laws invented by men.

14. We see also how the priesthood is fallen, and how many a poor priest is encumbered with a woman and children and burdened in his conscience, and no one does anything to help him, though he might very well be helped. Popes and bishops may let that be lost that is being lost, and that be destroyed which is being destroyed, I will save my conscience and open my mouth freely, let it vex popes and bishops or whoever it may be; therefore I say, According to the ordinances of Christ and His Apostles, every town should have a minister or bishop, as St. Paul plainly says (Titus i.), and this minister should not be forced to live without a lawful wife, but should be allowed to have one, as St. Paul writes, saying that "a bishop then must be blameless, the husband of one wife, . . . having his children in subjection with all gravity" (I Tim. iii.). For with St. Paul a bishop and a presbyter are the same thing, as St. Jerome also confirms. But as for the bishops that we now have, of these the Scriptures know nothing; they were instituted by common Christian ordinance, so that one might rule over many ministers.

Therefore we learn from the Apostle clearly, that every town should elect a pious learned citizen from the congregation and charge him with the office of minister; the congregation should support him, and he should be left at liberty to marry or not. He should have as assistants several priests and deacons, married or not, as they please, who should help him to govern the people and the congregation with sermons and the ministration of the sacraments, as is still the case in the Greek Church. Then afterwards, when there were so many persecutions and contentions

[30]Luther alludes here of course to the vow of celibacy, which was curiously styled the 'vow of chastity'; thus indirectly condemning marriage in general.

against heretics, there were many holy fathers who voluntarily abstained from the marriage state, that they might study more, and might be ready at all times for death and conflict. Now the Roman see has interfered of its own perversity, and has made a general law by which priests are forbidden to marry. This must have been at the instigation of the devil, as was foretold by St. Paul, saying that "there shall come teachers giving heed to seducing spirits, . . . forbidding to marry," etc. (I Tim. iv. 1, 2, *seq.*). This has been the cause of so much misery that it cannot be told, and has given occasion to the Greek Church to separate from us, and has caused infinite disunion, sin, shame, and scandal, like everything that the devil does or suggests. Now what are we to do?

My advice is to restore liberty, and to leave every man free to marry or not to marry. But if we did this we should have to introduce a very different rule and order for property; the whole canon law would be overthrown, and but few benefices would fall to Rome. I am afraid greed was a cause of this wretched, unchaste chastity, for the result of it was that every man wished to become a priest or to have his son brought up to the priesthood, not with the intention of living in chastity—for this could be done without the priestly state—but to obtain his worldly support without labour or trouble, contrary to God's command, "In the sweat of thy face shalt thou eat thy bread" (Gen. iii.); and they have given a colour to this commandment as though their work was praying and reading the mass. I am not here considering popes, bishops, canons, clergy, and monks who were not ordained by God; if they have laid burdens on themselves, they may bear them. I speak of the office of parish priest, which God ordained, who must rule a congregation with sermons and the ministration of the sacraments, and must live with them and lead a domestic life. These should have the liberty given them by a Christian council to marry and to avoid danger and sin. For as God has not bound them, no one may bind them, though he were an angel from heaven, let alone the Pope; and whatever is contrary to this in the canon law is mere idle talk and invention.

My advice further is, whoever henceforth is ordained priest, he should in no wise take the vow of chastity, but should protest to the bishop that he has no authority to demand this vow, and that it is a devilish tyranny to demand it. But if one is forced, or wishes to say, as some do, "so far as human frailty permits," let every man interpret that phrase as a plain negative, that is, "I do not promise chastity"; for "human frailty does not allow men to live an unmarried life," but only "angelic fortitude and celestial virtue." In this way he will have a clear conscience without any vow. I offer no opinion, one way or the other, whether those who have at present no wife should marry, or remain unmarried. This must be settled by the general order of the Church and by each man's discretion. But I will not conceal my honest counsel, nor withhold comfort from that unhappy crowd who now live in trouble with wife and children, and remain in shame, with a heavy conscience, hearing their wife called a priest's harlot, and the children bastards. And this I say frankly, in virtue of my good right.

There is many a poor priest free from blame in all other respects, except that he has succumbed to human frailty and come to shame with a woman, both minded in their hearts to live together always in conjugal fidelity, if only they could do so with a good conscience, though as it is they live in public shame. I say, these two are surely married before God. I say, moreover, that when two are so minded, and so come to live together, they should save their conscience; let the man take the woman as his lawful wife, and live with her faithfully as her husband, without considering whether the Pope approve or not, or whether it is forbidden by canon law, or temporal. The salvation of your soul is of more importance than their tyrannous, arbitrary, wicked laws, which are not necessary for salvation, nor ordained by God. You should do as the children of Israel did who stole from the Egyptians the wages they had earned, or as a servant steals his well-earned wages from a harsh master; in the same way do you also steal your wife and child from the Pope.

Let him who has faith enough to dare this only follow me

courageously: I will not mislead him. I may not have the Pope's authority, yet I have the authority of a Christian to help my neighbour and to warn him against his sins and dangers. And here there is good reason for doing so.

(a) It is not every priest that can do without a woman, not only on account of human frailty, but still more for his household. If therefore he takes a woman, and the Pope allows this, but will not let them marry, what is this but expecting a man and a woman to live together and not to fall? Just as if one were to set fire to straw, and command it should neither smoke nor burn.

(b) The Pope having no authority for such a command, any more than to forbid a man to eat and drink, or to digest, or to grow fat, no one is bound to obey it, and the Pope is answerable for every sin against it, for all the souls that it has brought to destruction, and for all the consciences that have been troubled and tormented by it. He has long deserved to be driven out of the world, so many poor souls has he strangled with this devil's rope, though I hope that God has shown many more mercy at their death than the Pope did in their life. No good has ever come and can ever come from the papacy and its laws.

(c) Even though the Pope's laws forbid it, still, after the married state has been entered, the Pope's laws are superseded, and are valid no longer, for God has commanded that no man shall put asunder husband and wife, and this commandment is far above the Pope's laws, and God's command must not be cancelled or neglected for the papal commands. It is true that mad lawyers have helped the Pope to invent impediments, or hindrances to marriage, and thus troubled, divided, and perverted the married state, destroying the commandments of God. What need I say further? In the whole body of the Pope's canon law, there are not two lines that can instruct a pious Christian, and so many false and dangerous ones that it were better to burn it.

But if you object that this would give offence, and that one must first obtain the Pope's dispensation, I answer that if there is any offence in it, it is the fault of the see of Rome, which has made unjust and unholy laws. It is no offence to God and the

Scriptures. Even where the Pope has power to grant dispensation for money by his covetous tyrannical laws, every Christian
has power to grant dispensation in the same matter for the sake
of Christ and the salvation of souls. For Christ has freed us from
all human laws, especially when they are opposed to God and
the salvation of souls, as St. Paul teaches (Gal. v. 1 and I Cor.
viii. 9, 10).

15. I must not forget the poor convents. The evil spirit, who
has troubled all estates of life by human laws, and made them
unendurable, has taken possession of some abbots, abbesses,
and prelates, and led them so to rule their brothers and sisters
that they do but go soon to hell, and live a wretched life even
upon earth, as is the case with all the devil's martyrs. For they
have reserved in confession all, or at least some, deadly sins,
which are secret, and from these no brother may on pain of excommunication and on his obedience absolve another. Now we
do not always find angels everywhere, but men of flesh and
blood, who would rather incur all excommunication and
menace than confess their secret sins to a prelate or the confessor
appointed for them; consequently they receive the Sacrament
with these sins on their conscience, by which they become *ir-
regular*[31] and suffer much misery. Oh blind shepherds! Oh
foolish prelates! Oh ravenous wolves! Now I say that in cases
where a sin is public and notorious it is only right that the
prelate alone should punish it, and such sins, and no others, he
may reserve and except for himself; over private sins he has no
authority, even though they may be the worst that can be committed or imagined. And if the prelate excepts these, he becomes
a tyrant and interferes with God's judgment.

Accordingly I advise these children, brothers and sisters: If
your superiors will not allow you to confess your secret sins to
whomsoever you will, then take them yourself, and confess them
to your brother or sister, to whomsoever you will; be absolved

---

[31] Luther uses the expression *irregulares,* which was applied to those monks
who were guilty of heresy, apostasy, transgression of the vow of chastity, etc.

and comforted, and then go or do what your wish or duty commands; only believe firmly that you have been absolved, and nothing more is necessary. And let not their threats of excommunication, or *irregularity,* or what not, trouble or disturb you; these only apply to public or notorious sins, if they are not confessed: you are not touched by them. How canst thou take upon thyself, thou blind prelate, to restrain private sins by thy threats? Give up what thou canst keep publicly; let God's judgment and mercy also have its place with thy inferiors. He has not given them into thy hands so completely as to have let them go out of His own; nay, thou hast received the smaller portion. Consider thy statutes as nothing more than thy statutes, and do not make them equal to God's judgment in heaven.

16. It were also right to abolish annual festivals, processions, and masses for the dead, or at least to diminish their number; for we evidently see that they have become no better than a mockery, exciting the anger of God and having no object but money-getting, gluttony, and carousals. How should it please God to hear the poor vigils and masses mumbled in this wretched way, neither read nor prayed? Even when they are properly read, it is not done freely for the love of God, but for the love of money and as payment of a debt. Now it is impossible that anything should please God or win anything from Him that is not done freely, out of love for Him. Therefore, as true Christians, we ought to abolish or lessen a practice that we see is abused, and that angers God instead of appeasing Him. I should prefer, and it would be more agreeable to God's will, and far better for a foundation, church, or convent, to put all the yearly masses and vigils together into one mass, so that they would every year celebrate, on one day, a true vigil and mass with hearty sincerity, devotion, and faith for all their benefactors. this would be better than their thousand upon thousand masses said every year, each for a particular benefactor, without devotion and faith. My dear fellow-Christians, God cares not for much prayer, but for good prayer. Nay, He condemns long and frequent prayers, saying, "Verily I say unto you, they have their

reward'' (Matt. vi. 2, *seq.*). But it is the greed that cannot trust God by which such practices are set up; it is afraid it will die of starvation.

17. One should also abolish certain punishments inflicted by the canon law, especially the interdict, which is doubtless the invention of the evil one. Is it not the mark of the devil to wish to better one sin by more and worse sins? It is surely a greater sin to silence God's word, and service, than if we were to kill twenty popes at once, not to speak of a single priest or of keeping back the goods of the Church. This is one of those gentle virtues which are learnt in the spiritual law; for the canon or spiritual law is so called because it comes from a spirit, not, however, from the Holy Spirit, but from the evil spirit.

Excommunication should not be used except where the Scriptures command it, that is, against those that have not the right faith, or that live in open sin, and not in matters of temporal goods. But now the case has been inverted: each man believes and lives as he pleases, especially those that plunder and disgrace others with excommunications; and all excommunications are now only in matters of worldly goods, for which we have no one to thank but the holy canonical injustice. But of all this I have spoken previously in a sermon.

The other punishments and penalties—suspension, irregularity, aggravation, reaggravation, deposition,[32] thundering, lightning, cursing, damning, and what not—all these should be buried ten fathoms deep in the earth, that their very name and memory may no longer live upon earth. The evil spirit, who was let loose by the spiritual law, has brought all this terrible plague and misery into the heavenly kingdom of the holy Church, and has thereby brought about nothing but the harm and destruction of souls, that we may well apply to it the words of Christ, ''But woe unto you, scribes and Pharisees, hypocrites! for you shut up

---

[32]Luther enumerates here the various grades of punishment inflicted on priests. The *aggravation* consisted of a threat of excommunication after a thrice-repeated admonition, whilst luther consequence of *reaggravation* was immediate excommunication.

the kingdom of heaven against men, for ye neither go in yourselves, neither suffer ye them that are entering to go in" (Matt.
xxiii. 13).

18. One should abolish all saints' days, keeping only Sunday.
But if it were desired to keep the festivals of Our Lady and the
greater saints, they should all be held on Sundays, or only in the
morning with the mass; the rest of the day being a working day.
My reason is this: with our present abuses of drinking, gam-
bling, idling, and all manner of sin, we vex God more on holy
days than on others. And the matter is just reversed; we have
made holy days unholy, and working days holy, and do no service, but great dishonour, to God and His saints with all our holy
days. There are some foolish prelates that think they have done
a good deed, if they establish a festival to St. Otilia or St. Bar-
bara, and the like, each in his own blind fashion, whilst he
would be doing a much better work to turn a saint's day into a
working day in honour of a saint.

Besides these spiritual evils, these saints' days inflict bodily injury on the common man in two ways: he loses a day's work,
and he spends more than usual, besides weakening his body and
making himself unfit for labour, as we see every day, and yet no
one tries to improve it. One should not consider whether the
Pope instituted these festivals, or whether we require his dispensation or permission. If anything is contrary to God's will and
harmful to men in body and soul, not only has every community, council, or government authority to prevent and abolish
such wrong without the knowledge or consent of pope or
bishop, but it is their duty, as they value their soul's salvation, to
prevent it, even though pope and bishop (that should be the first
to do so) are unwilling to see it stopped. And first of all we
should abolish church wakes, since they are nothing but taverns,
fairs, and gaming places, to the greater dishonour of God and
the damnation of souls. It is no good to make a talk about their
having had a good origin and being good works. Did not God
set aside His own law that He had given forth out of heaven
when He saw that it was abused, and does He not now reverse

every day what He has appointed, and destroy what He has made, on account of the same perverse misuse, as it is written in Psalm xviii. (ver. 26), "With the perverse Thou wilt show Thyself froward"?

19. The degrees of relationship in which marriage is forbidden must be altered, such as so-called spiritual relations[33] in the third and fourth degrees; and where the Pope at Rome can dispense in such matters for money, and make shameful bargains, every priest should have the power of granting the same dispensations freely for the salvation of souls. Would to God that all those things that have to be bought at Rome, for freedom from the golden snares of the canon law, might be given by any priest without payment, such as indulgences, letters of indulgences, letters of dispensation, mass letters, and all the other religious licences and knaveries at Rome by which the poor people are deceived and robbed! For if the Pope has the power to sell for money his golden snares, or canon nets (laws, I should say), much more has a priest the power to cancel them and to trample on them for God's sake. But if he has no such power, then the Pope can have no authority to sell them in his shameful fair.

Besides this, fasts must be made optional, and every kind of food made free, as is commanded in the Gospels (Matt. xv. 11). For whilst at Rome they laugh at fasts, they let us abroad consume oil which they would not think fit for greasing their boots, and then sell us the liberty of eating butter and other things, whereas the Apostle says that the Gospel has given us freedom in all such matters (I Cor. x. 25, *seq.*). But they have caught us in their canon law and have robbed us of this right, so that we have to buy it back from them; they have so terrified the consciences of the people that one cannot preach this liberty without rousing the anger of the people, who think the eating of butter to be a worse sin than lying, swearing, and unchastity. We may make of it what we will; it is but the work of man, and no good can ever come of it.

---

[33] Those, namely, between sponsors at baptism and their god-children.

20. The country chapels and churches must be destroyed, such as those to which the new pilgrimages have been set on foot: Wilsnack, Sternberg, Treves, the Grimmenthal, and now Ratisbon, and many others. Oh, what a reckoning there will be for those bishops that allow these inventions of the devil and make a profit out of them! They should be the first to stop it; they think that it is a godly, holy thing, and do not see that the devil does this to strengthen covetousness, to teach false beliefs, to weaken parish churches, to increase drunkenness and debauchery, to waste money and labour, and simply to lead the poor people by the nose. If they had only studied the Scriptures as much as their accursed canon law, they would know well how to deal with the matter.

The miracles performed there prove nothing, for the evil one can show also wonders, as Christ has taught us (Matt. xxiv. 24). If they took up the matter earnestly and forbade such doings, the miracles would soon cease: or if they were done by God, they would not be prevented by their commands. And if there were nothing else to prove that these are not works of God, it would be enough that people go about turbulently and irrationally like herds of cattle, which could not possibly come from God. God has not commanded it; there is no obedience, and no merit in it; and therefore it should be vigorously interfered with, and the people warned against it. For what is not commanded by God and goes beyond God's commandments is surely the devil's own work. In this way also the parish churches suffer: in that they are less venerated. In fine, these pilgrimages are signs of great want of faith in the people; for if they truly believed, they would find all things in their own churches, where they are commanded to go.

But what is the use of my speaking. Every man thinks only how he may get up such a pilgrimage in his own district, not caring whether the people believe and live rightly. The rulers are like the people: blind leaders of the blind. Where pilgrimages are a failure, they begin to glorify their saints, not to honour the saints, who are sufficiently honoured without them, but to cause a concourse, and to bring in money. Herein pope and bishops help them; it rains indulgences, and every one can afford to buy them: but what God has commanded no one cares for; no one runs after it, no one can afford any money for it. Alas for our blindness, that we not only suffer the devil to have his way with his phantoms, but support him! I wish one would leave the good saints alone, and not lead the poor people astray. What spirit gave the Pope authority to "glorify" the saints? Who tells him whether they are holy or not holy? Are there not enough sins on earth as it is but we must tempt God, interfere in His judgment, and make money-bags of His saints? Therefore my advice is to let the saints glorify themselves. Nay, God alone should be glorified, and every man should keep to his own parish, where he will profit more than in all these shrines, even if they were all put together into one shrine. Here a man finds baptism, the Sacrament, preaching, and his neighbour, and these are more than all the saints in heaven, for it is by God's word and sacrament that they have all been hallowed.

Our contempt for these great matters justifies God's anger in giving us over to the devil to lead us astray, to get up pilgrimages, to found churches and chapels, to glorify the saints, and to commit other like follies, by which we are led astray from the true faith into new false beliefs, just as He did in old time with the people of Israel, whom He led away from the Temple to countless other places, all the while in God's name, and with the appearance of holiness, against which all the prophets preached, suffering martyrdom for their words. But now no one preaches against it; for if he did, bishops, popes, priests, and monks would perchance combine to martyr him. In this way Antonius of Florence and many others are made saints, so that their holiness may serve to produce glory and wealth, which served before to the honour of God and as a good example alone.

Even if this glorification of the saints had been good once, it is not good now, just as many other things were good once and are now occasion of offence and injurious, such as holidays, ecclesiastical treasures and ornaments. For it is evident that what is aimed at in the glorification of saints is not the glory of God nor the bettering of Christendom, but money and fame alone; one Church wishes to have an advantage over another, and would be sorry to see another Church enjoying the same advantages. In this way they have in these latter days abused the goods of the Church so as to gain the goods of the world; so that everything, and even God Himself, must serve their avarice. Moreover, these privileges cause nothing but dissensions and worldly pride; one Church being different from the rest, they despise or magnify one another, whereas all goods that are of God should be common to all, and should serve to produce unity. This, too, is much liked by the Pope, who would be sorry to see all Christians equal and at one with one another.

Here must be added that one should abolish, or treat as of no account, or give to all Churches alike, the licences, bulls, and whatever the Pope sells at his flaying-ground at Rome. For if he sells or gives to Wittenberg, to Halle, to Venice, and above all, to his own city of Rome, permissions, privileges, indulgences, graces, advantages, faculties, why does he not give them to all Churches alike? Is it not his duty to do all that he can for all Christians without reward, solely for God's sake, nay even to shed his blood for them? Why then, I should like to know, does he give or sell these things to one Church and not to another? Or does this accursed gold make a difference in his Holiness's eyes between Christians who all alike have baptism, Gospel, faith, Christ, God, and all things? Do they wish us to be blind, when our eyes can see, to be fools, when we have reason, that we should worship this greed knavery, and delusion? He is a shepherd, forsooth—so long as you have money, no further; and yet they are not ashamed to practise all this knavery right and left with their bulls. They care only for that accursed gold, and for nought besides.

Therefore my advice is this: If this folly is not done away with, let all pious Christians open their eyes, and not be deceived by these Romish bulls and seals and all their specious pretences; let them stop at home in their own churches, and be satisfied with their baptism, Gospel, faith, Christ, and God (who is everywhere the same), and let the Pope continue to be a blind leader of the blind. Neither pope nor angel can give you as much as God gives you in your own parish; nay, he only leads you away from God's gifts, which you have for nothing, to his own gifts, which you must buy, giving you lead for gold, skin for meat, strings for a purse, wax for honey, words for goods, the letter for the spirit, as you can see for yourselves though you will not perceive it. If you try to ride to heaven on the Pope's wax and parchment, your carriage will soon break down, and you will fall into hell, not in God's name.

Let this be a fixed rule for you: Whatever has to be bought of the Pope is neither good, nor of God. For whatever comes from God is not only given freely, but all the world is punished and condemned for not accepting it freely. So is it with the Gospel and the works of God. We have deserved to be led into these errors, because we have despised God's holy word and the grace of baptism; as St. Paul says, "And for this cause God shall send them strong delusion, that they should believe a lie, that they all might be damned who believed not the truth, but had pleasure in unrighteousness" (2 Thess. ii. 11, 12).

21. It is one of the most urgent necessities to abolish all begging in Christendom. No one should go about begging among Christians. It would not be hard to do this, if we attempted it with good heart and courage: each town should support its own poor and should not allow strange beggars to come in, whatever they may call themselves, pilgrims or mendicant monks. Every town could feed its own poor; and if it were too small, the people in the neighbouring villages should be called upon to contribute. As it is, they have to support many knaves and vagabonds under the name of beggars. If they did what I propose, they would at least know who were really poor or not.

There should also be an overseer or guardian who should know all the poor, and should inform the town-council, or the priest, of their requirements; or some other similar provision might be made. There is no occupation, in my opinion, in which there is so much knavery and cheating as among beggars; which could easily be done away with. This general, unrestricted begging is, besides, injurious for the common people. I estimate that of the five or six orders of mendicant monks each one visits every place more than six or seven times in the year; then there are the common beggars, emissaries, and pilgrims; in this way I calculate every city has a blackmail levied on it about sixty times a year, not counting rates and taxes paid to the civil government and the useless robberies of the Roman see; so that it is to my mind one of the greatest of God's miracles how we manage to live and support ourselves.

Some may think that in this way the poor would not be well cared for, and that such great stone houses and convents would not be built, and not so plentifully, and I think so too. Nor is it necessary. If a man will be poor, he should not be rich; if he will be rich, let him put his hand to the plough, and get wealth himself out of the earth. It is enough to provide decently for the poor, that they may not die of cold and hunger. It is not right that one should work that another may be idle, and live ill that another may live well, as is now the perverse abuse, for St. Paul says, "If any would not work, neither should he eat" (2 Thess. iii. 10). God has not ordained that any one should live of the goods of others, except priests and ministers alone, as St. Paul says (I Cor. ix. 14), for their spiritual work's sake, as also Christ says to the Apostles, "The labourer is worthy of his hire" (Luke x. 7).

22. It is also to be feared that the *many masses* that have been founded in convents and foundations, instead of doing any good, arouse God's anger; wherefore it would be well to endow no more masses and to abolish many of those that have been endowed; for we see that they are only looked upon as sacrifices and good works, though in truth they are sacraments like baptism and confession, and as such profit him only that receives them. But now the custom obtains of saying masses for the living and the dead, and everything is based upon them. This is the reason why there are so many, and that they have come to be what we see.

But perhaps all this is a new and unheard-of doctrine, especially in the eyes of those that fear to lose their livelihood, if these masses were abolished. I must therefore reserve what I have to say on this subject until men have arrived at a truer understanding of the mass, its nature and use. The mass has, alas! for so many years been turned into means of gaining a livelihood, that I should advise a man to become a shepherd, a labourer, rather than a priest or monk, unless he knows what the mass is.

All this, however, does not apply to the old foundations and chapters, which were doubtless founded in order that since, according to the custom of Germany, all the children of nobles cannot be land-owners and rulers, they should be provided for in these foundations, and these serve God freely, study, and become learned themselves, and help others to acquire learning. I am speaking only of the new foundations, endowed for prayers and masses, by the example of which the old foundations have become burdened with the like prayers and masses, making them of very little, if of any, use. Through God's righteous punishment, they have at last come down to the dregs, as they deserve—that is, to the noise of singers and organs, and cold, spiritless masses, with no end but to gain and spend the money due to them. Popes, bishops, and doctors should examine and report on such things; as it is they are the guiltiest, allowing anything that brings them money; the blind ever leading the blind. This comes of covetousness and the canon law.

It must, moreover, not be allowed in future that one man should have more than one endowment or prebend. He should be content with a moderate position in life, so that others may have something besides himself; and thus we must put a stop to the excuses of those that say that they must have more than one office to enable them to live in their proper station. It is possible to estimate one's "proper station" in such a way that a whole kingdom would not suffice to maintain it. So it is that covetousness and want of faith in God go hand in hand, and often men take for the requirements of their "proper station" what is mere covetousness and want of faith.

23. As for the fraternities, together with indulgences, letters of indulgence, dispensations for Lent, and masses, and all the rest of such things, let them all be drowned and abolished; there is no good in them at all. If the Pope has the authority to grant dispensation in the matter of eating butter and hearing masses, let him allow priests to do the same; he has no right to take the power from them. I speak also of the fraternities in which indulgences, masses, and good works are distributed. My friend, in baptism you joined a fraternity of which Christ, the angels, and saints, and all Christians are members; be true to this, and satisfy it, and you will have fraternities enough. Let others make what show they wish; they are as counters compared to coins. But if there were a fraternity that subscribed money to feed the poor or to help others in any way, this would be good, and it would have its indulgence and its deserts in heaven. But now they are good for nothing but gluttony and drunkenness.

First of all we should expel from all German lands the Pope's legates, with their faculties, which they sell to us for much money, though it is all knavery—as, for instance, their taking money for making goods unlawfully acquired to be good, for freeing from oaths, vows, and bonds, thus destroying and teaching others to destroy truth and faith mutually pledged, saying the Pope has authority to do so. It is the evil spirit that bids them talk thus, and so they sell us the devil's teaching, and take money for teaching us sins and leading us to hell.

If there were nothing else to show that the Pope is antichrist, this would be enough. Dost thou hear this, O Pope! not the most holy, but the most sinful? Would that God would hurl thy chair headlong from heaven, and cast it down into the abyss of hell! Who gave you the power to exalt yourself above your God; to break and to loose what He has commanded; to teach Christians, more especially Germans, who are of noble nature, and are famed in all histories for uprightness and truth, to be false, unfaithful, perjured, treacherous, and wicked? God has commanded to keep faith and observe oaths even with enemies; you dare to cancel this command, laying it down in your heretical, anti-Christian decretals that you have power to do so; and through your mouth and your pen Satan lies as he never lied before, teaching you to twist and pervert the Scriptures according to your own arbitrary will. O Lord Christ, look down upon this; let Thy day of judgment come and destroy the devil's lair at Rome. Behold him of whom St. Paul spoke (2 Thess. ii. 3, 4) that he should exalt himself above Thee and sit in Thy Church, showing himself as God—the man of sin and the child of damnation. What else does the Pope's power do but teach and strengthen sin and wickedness, leading souls to damnation in Thy name?

The children of Israel in old times were obliged to keep the oath that they had sworn, in ignorance and error, to the Gibeonites, their enemies; and King Zedekiah was destroyed utterly, with his people, because he broke the oath that he had sworn to the King of Babylon; and among us, a hundred years ago, the noble King Ladislaus V. of Poland and Hungary, was slain by the Turk, with so many of his people, because he allowed himself to be misled by papal legates and cardinals and broke the good and useful treaty that he had made with the Turk. The pious Emperor Sigismond had no good fortune after the Council of Constance, in which he allowed the knaves to violate the safe-conduct that he had promised to John Huss and Jerome; from this has followed all the miserable strife between Bohemia and ourselves. And in our own time, God help us! how much Christian blood has been shed on account of the oath and bond which Pope Julius made and unmade between the Emperor Maximilian and King Louis of France! How can I tell all the misery the popes have caused by such devilish insolence, claiming the power of breaking oaths between great lords, causing a shameful scandal for the sake of money? I hope the day of judgment is at hand; things cannot and will not become worse than the dealings of the Roman chair. The Pope treads God's commandments under foot and exalts his own; if this is not antichrist, I do not know what is. But of this, and to more purpose, another time.

24. It is high time to take up earnestly and truthfully the cause of the Bohemians, to unite them with ourselves and ourselves with them, so that all mutual accusations, envy, and hatred may cease. I will be the first, in my folly, to give my opinion, with all due deference to those of better understanding.

First of all, we must honestly confess the truth, without attempting self-justification, and own one thing to the Bohemians, namely that John Huss and Jerome of Prague were burnt at Constance in violation of the papal, Christian, and imperial oath and safe-conduct, and that thus God's commandment was broken and the Bohemians excited to great anger. And though they may have deserved such great wrong and disobedience to God on our part, they were not obliged to approve it and think it right. Nay, even now they should run any danger of life and limb rather than own that it is right to break an imperial, papal, Christian safe-conduct and act faithlessly in opposition to it. Therefore, though the Bohemians may be to blame for their impatience, yet the Pope and his followers are most to blame for all the misery, all the error and destruction of souls, that followed this council of Constance.

It is not my intention here to judge John Huss's belief and to defend his errors, although my understanding has not been able to find any error in him, and I would willingly believe that men who violated a safe-conduct and God's commandment (doubtless possessed rather by the evil spirit than by the Spirit of God) were unable to judge well or to condemn with truth. No one can imagine that the Holy Ghost can break God's commandments; no one can deny that it is breaking God's commandments to violate faith and a safe-conduct, even though it were promised to the devil himself, much more then in the case of a heretic; it is also notorious that a safe-conduct was promised to John Huss and the Bohemians, and that the promise was broken and Huss was burnt. I have no wish to make a saint or a martyr of John Huss (as some Bohemians do), though I own that he was treated unjustly, and that his books and his doctrines were wrongfully condemned; for God's judgments are inscrutable and terrible, and none but Himself may reveal or explain them.

All I say is this: Granting he was a heretic, however bad he may have been, yet he was burnt unjustly and in violation of God's commandments, and we must not force the Bohemians to approve this, if we wish ever to be at one with them. Plain truth must unite us, not obstinacy. It is no use to say, as they said at the time, that a safe-conduct need not be kept, if promised to a heretic; that is as much as to say, one may break God's commandments in order to keep God's commandments. They were infatuated and blinded by the devil, that they could not see what they said or did. God has commanded us to observe a safe-conduct; and this we must do though the world should perish: much more then where it is only a question of a heretic being set free. We should overcome heretics with books, not with fire, as the old Fathers did. If there were any skill in overcoming heretics with fire, the executioner would be the most learned doctor in the world; and there would be no need to study, but he that could get another into his power could burn him.

Besides this, the Emperor and the pinces should send to Bohemia serveral pious, learned bishops and doctors, but, for their life, no cardinal or legate or inquisitor, for such people are far too unlearned in all Christian matters, and do not seek the salvation of souls; but, like all the papal hypocrites, they seek only their own glory, profit, and honour; they were also the leaders in that calamitous affair at Constance. But those envoys should inquire into the faith of the Bohemians, to ascertain whether it would be possible to unite all their sects into one. Moreover, the Pope should (for their souls' sake) for a time abandon his supremacy and, in accordance with the statutes of the Nicene Council, allow the Bohemians to choose for themselves an archbishop of Prague, this choice to be confirmed by the Bishops of Olmutz in Moravia or of Gran in Hungary, or the Bishop of Gnesen in Poland, or the Bishop of Magdeburg in Germany. It is enough that it be confirmed by one or two of these bishops, as in the time of St. Cyprian. And the Pope has no authority to forbid it; if he forbids it, he acts as a wolf and a tyrant, and no one should obey him, but answer his excommunication by excommunicating him.

Yet if, for the honour of the chair of St. Peter, any one prefers to do this with the Pope's knowledge, I do not object, provided that the Bohemians do not pay a farthing for it, and that the Pope do not bind them a single hair's-breadth, or subject them to his tyranny by oath, as he does all other bishops, against God and justice. If he is not satisfied with the honour of his assent being asked, leave him alone, by all means, with his own rights, laws, and tyrannies; be content with the election, and let the blood of all the souls that are in danger be upon his head. For no man may countenance wrong, and it is enough to show respect to tyranny. If we cannot do otherwise, we may consider the popular election and consent as equal to a tyrannical confirmation; but I hope this will not be necessary. Sooner or later some Romans, or pious bishops and learned men, must perceive and avert the Pope's tyranny.

I do not advise that they be forced to abandon the Sacrament in both kinds, for it is neither unchristian nor heretical. They should be allowed to continue in their present way; but the new bishop must see that there be no dissensions about this matter, and they must learn that neither practice is actually wrong, just as there need be no disputes about the priests not wearing the same dress as the laity. In the same way, if they do not wish to submit to the canon laws of the Roman Church, we must not force them, but we must content ourselves with seeing that they live in faith and according to the Scriptures. For Christian life and Christian faith may very well exist without the Pope's unbearable laws; nay, they cannot well exist until there are fewer of those laws or none. Our baptism has freed us and made us subject to God's word alone; why then should we suffer a man to make us the slaves of his words? As St. Paul says, "Stand fast therefore in the liberty wherewith Christ hath made us free, and be not entangled again with the yoke of bondage" (Gal. v. 1).

If I knew that the only error of the Hussites[34] was that they believe that in the Sacrament of the altar there is true bread and wine, though under it the body and the blood of Christ—if, I say, this were their only error, I should not condemn them; but let the Bishop of Prague see to this. For it is not an article of faith that in the Sacrament there is no bread and wine in substance and nature, which is a delusion of St. Thomas and the Pope; but it is an article of faith that in the natural bread and wine there is Christ's true flesh and blood. We should accordingly tolerate the views of both parties until they are at one; for there is not much danger whether you believe there is or there is not bread in the Sacrament. For we have to suffer many forms of belief and order that do not injure the faith; but if they believe otherwise, it would be better not to unite with them, and yet to instruct them in the truth.

All other errors and dissensions to be found in Bohemia should be tolerated until the Archbishop has been reinstated, and has succeeded in time in uniting the whole people in one harmonious doctrine. We shall never unite them by force, by driving or hurrying them. We must be patient, and use gentleness. Did not Christ have to walk with His disciples, suffering their unbelief, until they believed in His resurrection? If they had but once more a regular bishop and good government without Romish tyranny, I think matters would mend.

The temporal possessions of the Church should not be too strictly claimed; but since we are Christians and bound to help one another, we have the right to give them these things for the sake of unity, and to let them keep them, before God and the world; for Christ says, "Where two or three are gathered together in My name, there am I in the midst of them." Would to God we helped on both sides to bring about this unity, giving our hands one to the other in brotherly humility, not insisting on our authority or our rights! Love is more, and more necessary,

---

[34]Luther uses here the word *Pikarden,* which is a corruption of *Begharden,* i. e. "Beghards," a nickname frequently applied in those days to the Hussites.

than the papacy at Rome, which is without love, and love can exist without the papacy. I hope I have done my best for this end. If the Pope or his followers hinder this good work, they will have to give an account of their actions for having, against the love of God, sought their own advantage more than their neighbours'. The Pope should abandon his papacy, all his possessions and honours, if he could save a soul by so doing. But he would rather see the world go to ruin than give up a hair's-breadth of the power he has usurped; and yet he would be our most holy father. Herewith I am excused.

25. The universities also require a good, sound reformation. I must say this, let it vex whom it may. The fact is that whatever the papacy has ordered or instituted is only designed for the propagation of sin and error. What are the universities, as at present ordered, but, as the book of Maccabees says, "schools of 'Greek fashion' and 'heathenish manners'" (2 Macc. iv. 12, 13), full of dissolute living, where very little is taught of the Holy Scriptures and of the Christian faith, and the blind heathen teacher, Aristotle, rules even further than Christ? Now, my advice would be that the books of Aristotle, the *Physics,* the *Metaphysics, Of the Soul, Ethics,* which have hitherto been considered the best, be altogether abolished, with all others that profess to treat of nature, though nothing can be learned from them, either of natural or of spiritual things. Besides, no one has been able to understand his meaning, and much time has been wasted and many noble souls vexed with much useless labour, study, and expense. I venture to say that any potter has more knowledge of natural things than is to be found in these books. My heart is grieved to see how many of the best Christians this accursed, proud, knavish heathen has fooled and led astray with his false words. God sent him as a plague for our sins.

Does not the wretched man in his best book, *Of the Soul,* teach that the soul dies with the body, though many have tried to save him with vain words, as if we had not the Holy Scriptures to teach us fully of all things of which Aristotle had not the slightest perception? Yet this dead heathen has conquered, and has hindered and almost suppressed the books of the living God; so that, when I see all this misery I cannot but think that the evil spirit has introduced this study.

Then there is the *Ethics*, which is accounted one of the best, though no book is more directly contrary to God's will and the Christian virtues. Oh that such books could be kept out of the reach of all Christians! Let no one object that I say too much, or speak without knowledge. My friend, I know of what I speak. I know Aristotle as well as you or men like you. I have read him with more understanding than St. Thomas or Scotus, which I may say without arrogance, and can prove if need be. It matters not that so many great minds have exercised themselves in these matters for many hundred years. Such objections do not affect me as they might have done once, since it is plain as day that many more errors have existed for many hundred years in the world and the universities.

I would, however, gladly consent that Aristotle's books of Logic, Rhetoric, and Poetry, should be retained, or they might be usefully studied in a condensed form, to practise young people in speaking and preaching; but the notes and comments should be abolished, and, just as Cicero's Rhetoric is read without note or comment, Aristotle's Logic should be read without such long commentaries. But now neither speaking nor preaching is taught out of them, and they are used only for disputation and toilsomeness. Besides this, there are languages—Latin, Greek, and Hebrew—the mathematics, history; which I recommend to men of higher understanding: and other matters, which will come of themselves, if they seriously strive after reform. And truly it is an important matter, for it concerns the teaching and training of Christian youths and of our noble people, in whom Christianity still abides. Therefore I think that pope and emperor could have no better task than the reformation of the universities, just as there is nothing more devilishly mischievous than an unreformed university.

Physicians I would leave to reform their own faculty; lawyers and theologians I take under my charge, and say firstly that it would be right to abolish the canon law entirely, from beginning to end, more especially the decretals. We are taught quite sufficiently in the Bible how we ought to act; all this study only prevents the study of the Scriptures, and for the most part it is tainted with covetousness and pride. And even though there were some good in it, it should nevertheless be destroyed, for the Pope, having the canon law *in scrinio pectoris*,[35] all further study is useless and deceitful. At the present time the canon law is not to be found in the books, but in the whims of the Pope and his sycophants. You may have settled a matter in the best possible way according to the canon law, but the Pope has his *scrinium pectoris,* to which all law must bow in all the world. Now this *scrinium* is oftentimes directed by some knave and the devil himself, whilst it boasts that it is directed by the Holy Ghost. This is the way they treat Christ's poor people, imposing many laws and keeping none, forcing others to keep them or to free themselves by money.

Therefore, since the Pope and his followers have cancelled the whole canon law, despising it and setting their own will above all the world, we should follow them and reject the books. Why should we study them to no purpose? We should never be able to know the Pope's caprice, which has now become the canon law. Let it fall then in God's name, after having risen in the devil's name. Let there be henceforth no *doctor decretorum,* but let them all be *doctores scrinii papalis,* that is, the Pope's sycophants. They say that there is no better temporal government than among the Turks, though they have no canon nor civil law, but only their Koran; we must at least own that there is no worse government than ours, with its canon and civil law, for no estate lives according to the Scriptures, or even according to natural reason.

The civil law, too, good God! what a wilderness it is become! It is, indeed, much better, more skilful, and more honest than the canon law, of which nothing is good but the name. Still there

[35] In the shrine of his heart.

is far too much of it. Surely good governors, in addition to the Holy Scriptures, would be law enough; as St. Paul says, ''Is it so that there is not a wise man among you, no, not one that shall be able to judge between his brethren?'' (I Cor. vi. 5). I think also that the common law and the usage of the country should be preferred to the law of the empire, and that the law of the empire should only be used in cases of necessity. And would to God, that, as each land has its own peculiar character and nature, they could all be governed by their own simple laws, just as they were governed before the law of the empire was devised, and as many are governed even now! Elaborate and far-fetched laws are only burdensome to the people, and a hindrance rather than a help to business. But I hope that others have thought of this, and considered it to more purpose than I could.

Our worthy theologians have saved themselves much trouble and labour by leaving the Bible alone and only reading the Sentences.[36] I should have thought that young theologians might begin by studying the Sentences, and that doctors should study the Bible. Now they invert this: the Bible is the first thing they study; this ceases with the Bachelor's degree; the Sentences are the last, and these they keep forever with the Doctor's degree, and this, too, under such sacred obligation that one that is not a priest may read the Bible, but a priest must read the Sentences; so that, as far as I can see, a married man might be a doctor in the Bible, but not in the Sentences. How should we prosper so long as we act so perversely, and degrade the Bible, the holy word of God? Besides this, the Pope orders with many stringent words that his laws be read and used in schools and courts; while the law of the Gospel is but little considered. The result is that in schools and courts the Gospel lies dusty underneath the benches, so that the Pope's mischievous laws may alone be in force.

Since then we hold the name and title of teachers of the Holy

---

[36]Luther refers here to the ''Sentences'' of *Petrus Lombardus,* the so-called *magister sententiarum,* which formed the basis of all dogmatic interpretation from about the middle of the twelfth century down to the Reformation.

Scriptures, we should verily be forced to act according to our title, and to teach the Holy Scriptures and nothing else. Although, indeed, it is a proud, presumptuous title for a man to proclaim himself teacher of the Scriptures, still it could be suffered, if the works confirmed the title. But as it is, under the rule of the Sentences, we find among theologians more human and heathenish fallacies than true holy knowledge of the Scriptures. What then are we to do? I know not, except to pray humbly to God to give us Doctors of Theology. Doctors of Arts, of Medicine, of Law, of the Sentences, may be made by popes, emperors, and the universities; but of this we may be certain: a Doctor of the Holy Scriptures can be made by none but the Holy Ghost, as Christ says, "They shall all be taught of God" (John vi. 45). Now the Holy Ghost does not consider red caps or brown, or any other pomp, nor whether we are young or old, layman or priest, monk or secular, virgin or married; nay, He once spoke by an ass against the prophet that rode on it. Would to God we were worthy of having such doctors given us, be they laymen or priests, married or unmarried! But now they try to force the Holy Ghost to enter into popes, bishops, or doctors, though there is no sign to show that He is in them.

We must also lessen the number of theological books, and choose the best, for it is not the number of books that makes the learned man, nor much reading, but good books often read, however few, makes a man learned in the Scriptures and pious. Even the Fathers should only be read for a short time as an introduction to the Scriptures. As it is we read nothing else, and never get from them into the Scriptures, as if one should be gazing at the signposts and never follow the road. These good Fathers wished to lead us into the Scriptures by their writings, whereas we lead ourselves out by them, though the Scriptures are our vineyard, in which we should all work and exercise ourselves.

Above all, in schools of all kinds the chief and most common lesson should be the Scriptures, and for young boys the Gospel; and would to God each town had also a girls' school, in which girls might be taught the Gospel for an hour daily, either in German or Latin! In truth, schools, monasteries, and convents were founded for this purpose, and with good Christian intentions, as we read concerning St. Agnes and other saints[37]; then were there holy virgins and martyrs; and in those times it was well with Christendom; but now it has been turned into nothing but praying and singing. Should not every Christian be expected by his ninth or tenth year to know all the holy Gospels, containing as they do his very name and life? A spinner or a seamstress teaches her daughter her trade while she is young, but now even the most learned prelates and bishops do not know the Gospel.

Oh, how badly we treat all these poor young people that are entrusted to us for discipline and instruction! and a heavy reckoning shall we have to give for it that we keep them from the word of God; their fate is that described by Jeremiah: "Mine eyes do fail with tears, my bowels are troubled, my liver is poured upon the earth, for the destruction of the daughter of my people, because the children and the sucklings swoon in the streets of the city. They say to their mothers, Where is corn and wine? when they swooned as the wounded in the streets of the city, when their soul was poured out into their mothers' bosom" (Lam. ii. 11, 12). We do not perceive all this misery, how the young folk are being pitifully corrupted in the midst of Christendom, all for want of the Gospel, which we should always read and study with them.

However, even if the high schools studied the Scriptures diligently we should not send every one to them, as we do now, when nothing is considered but numbers, and every man wishes to have a Doctor's title; we should only send the aptest pupils, well prepared in the lower schools. This should be seen to by princes or the magistrates of the towns, and they should take care none but apt pupils be sent. But where the Holy Scriptures are not the rule, I advise no one to send his child. Everything must perish where God's word is not studied unceasingly; and so

[37]See above, pp. 59, *seq.*

we see what manner of men there are now in the high schools, and all this is the fault of no one but of the Pope, the bishops, and the prelates, to whom the welfare of the young has been entrusted. For the high schools should only train men of good understanding in the Scriptures, who wish to become bishops and priests, and to stand at our head against heretics and the devil and all the world. But where do we find this? I greatly fear the high schools are nothing but great gates of hell, unless they diligently study the Holy Scriptures and teach them to the young people.

26. I know well the Romish mob will object and loudly pretend that the Pope took the holy Roman empire from the Greek emperor and gave it to Germany, for which honour and favour he is supposed to deserve submission and thanks and all other kinds of returns from the Germans. For this reason they will perhaps assume to oppose all attempts to reform them, and will let no regard be paid to anything but those donations of the Roman empire. This is also the reason why they have so arbitrarily and proudly persecuted and oppressed many good emperors, so that it were pity to tell, and with the same cleverness have they made themselves lords of all the temporal power and authority, in violation of the holy Gospel; and accordingly I must speak of this matter also.

There is no doubt that the true Roman empire, of which the prophets (Num. xxiv. 24 and Daniel ii. 44) spoke, was long ago destroyed, as Balaam clearly foretold, saying, "And ships shall come from the coast of Chittim, and shall afflict Asshur, and shall afflict Eber, and he also shall perish for ever" (Num. xxiv. 24).[38] And this was done by the Goths, and more especially since the empire of the Turks was formed, about one thousand years ago, and so gradually Asia and Africa were lost, and subsequently France, Spain, and finally Venice arose, so that Rome

---

[38]Luther here follows the Vulgate, translating the above verse: "Es werden die Römer kommen und die Juden verstören: und hernach werden sie auch untergehen."

retains no part of its former power.

Since then the Pope could not force the Greeks and the emperor at Constantinople, who is the hereditary Roman emperor, to obey his will, he invented this device to rob him of his empire and title, and to give it to the Germans, who were at that time strong and of good repute, in order that they might take the power of the Roman empire and hold it of the Pope; and this is what actually has happened. It was taken from the emperor at Constantinople, and the name and title were given to us Germans, and therewith we became subject to the Pope, and he has built up a new Roman empire on the Germans. For the other empire, the original, came to an end long ago, as was said above.

Thus the Roman see has got what it wished: Rome has been taken possession of, and the German emperor driven out and bound by oaths not to dwell in Rome. He is to be Roman emperor and nevertheless not to dwell in Rome, and, moreover, always to depend on the Pope and his followers, and to do their will. We are to have the title, and they are to have the lands and the cities. For they have always made our simplicity the tool of their pride and tyranny, and they consider us as stupid Germans, to be deceived and fooled by them as they choose.

Well, for our Lord God it is a small thing to toss kingdoms and principalities hither and thither; He is so free with them that He will sometimes take a kingdom from a good man and give it to a knave, sometimes through the treachery of false, wicked men, sometimes by inheritance, as we read concerning Persia, Greece, and nearly all kingdoms; and Daniel says, "Wisdom and might are His; and He changes the times and the seasons, and He removeth kings and setteth up kings" (Dan. ii. 20, 21). Therefore no one need think it a grand matter if he has a kingdom given to him, especially if he be a Christian; and so we Germans need not be proud of having had a new Roman empire given us. For in His eyes it is a poor gift, that He sometimes gives to the least deserving, as Daniel says, "And all the inhabitants of the earth are reputed as nothing; and He does according to His will in the army of heaven, and among the inhabitants of the earth'' (Dan. iv. 35).

Now, although the Pope has violently and unjustly robbed the true emperor of the Roman empire, or its name, and has given it to us Germans, yet it is certain that God has used the Pope's wickedness to give the German nation this empire and to raise up a new Roman empire, that exists now, after the fall of the old empire. We gave the Pope no cause for this action, nor did we understand his false aims and schemes; but still, through the craft and knavery of the popes, we have, alas! all too dearly, paid the price of this empire with incalculable bloodshed, with the loss of our liberty, with the robbery of our wealth, especially of our churches and benefices, and with unspeakable treachery and insult. We have the empire in name, but the Pope has our wealth, our honour, our bodies, lives, and souls and all that we have. This was the way to deceive the Germans, and to deceive them by shuffling. What the popes wished was to become emperors; and as they could not do this, they put themselves above the emperors.

Since, then, we have received this empire through God's providence and the schemes of evil men, without our fault, I would not advise that we should give it up, but that we should govern it honestly, in the fear of God, so long as He is pleased to let us hold it. For, as I have said, it is no matter to Him how a kingdom is come by, but He will have it duly governed. If the popes took it from others dishonestly, we at least did not come by it dishonestly. It was given to us through evil men, under the will of God, to whom we have more regard than the false intentions of the popes, who wished to be emperors and more than emperors and to fool and mock us with the name.

The King of Babylon obtained his kingdom by force and robbery; yet God would have it governed by the holy princes Daniel, Ananias, Asarias, and Misael. Much more then does He require this empire to be governed by the Christian princes of Germany, though the Pope may have stolen, or robbed, or newly fashioned it. It is all God's ordering, which came to pass before we knew of it.

Therefore the Pope and his followers have no reason to boast that they did a great kindness to the German nation in giving them this Roman empire; firstly, because they intended no good to us, in the matter, but only abused our simplicity to strengthen their own power against the Roman emperor at Constantinople, from whom, against God and justice, the Pope has taken what he had no right to.

Secondly, the Pope sought to give the empire, not to us, but to himself, and to become lord over all our power, liberty, wealth, body and soul, and through us over all the world, if God had not prevented it, as he plainly says in his decretals, and has tried with many mischievous tricks in the case of many German emperors. Thus we Germans have been taught in plain German: whilst we expected to become lords, we have become the servants of the most crafty tyrants; we have the name, title, and arms of the empire, but the Pope has the treasure, authority, law, and freedom; thus, whilst the Pope eats the kernel, he leaves us the empty shells to play with.

Now may God help us (who, as I have said, assigned us this kingdom through crafty tyrants, and charged us to govern it) to act according to our name, title, and arms, and to secure our freedom, and thus let the Romans see at last what we have received of God through them. If they boast that they have given us an empire, well, be it so, by all means; then let the Pope give up Rome, all he has of the empire, and free our country from his unbearable taxes and robberies, and give back to us our liberty, authority, wealth, honour, body, and soul, rendering to the empire those things that are the empire's, so as to act in accordance with his words and pretences.

But if he will not do this, what game is he playing with all his falsehoods and pretences? Was it not enough to lead this great people by the nose for so many hundred years? Because the Pope crowns or makes the Emperor, it does not follow that he is above him; for the prophet, St. Samuel, anointed and crowned King Saul and David, at God's command, and was yet subject to them. And the prophet Nathan anointed King Solomon, and yet was not placed over him; moreover, St. Elisha let one of his servants anoint King Jehu of Israel, yet they obeyed him. And it has never yet happened in the whole world that any one was above the king because he consecrated or crowned him, except in the case of the Pope.

Now he is himself crowned pope by three cardinals; yet they are subject to him, and he is above them. Why, then, contrary to his own example and to the doctrine and practice of the whole world and the Scriptures, should he exalt himself above the temporal authorities, and the empire, for no other reason than that he crowns, and consecrates the Emperor? It suffices that he is above him in all divine matters—that is, in preaching, teaching, and the ministration of the Sacrament—in which matters, however, every priest or bishop is above all other men, just as St. Ambrose in his chair was above the Emperor Theodosius, and the prophet Nathan above David, and Samuel above Saul. Therefore let the German emperor be a true free emperor, and let not his authority or his sword be overborne by these blind pretences of the Pope's sycophants, as if they were to be exceptions, and be above the temporal sword in all things.

27. Let this be enough about the faults of the spiritual estate, though many more might be found, if the matter were properly considered; we must now consider the defects of the temporal estates. In the first place, we require a general law and consent of the German nation against profusion and extravagance in dress, which is the cause of so much poverty among the nobles and the people. Surely God has given to us, as to other nations, enough wool, fur, flax, and whatever else is required for the decent clothing of every class; and it cannot be necessary to spend such enormous sums for silk, velvet, cloth of gold, and all other kinds of outlandish stuff. I think that even if the Pope did not rob us Germans with his unbearable taxes, we should be robbed more than enough by these secret thieves, the dealers in silk and velvet. As it is, we see that every man wishes to be every other man's equal, and that this causes and increases pride and envy among us, as we deserve, all which would cease, with many

other misfortunes, if our self-will would but let us be gratefully content with what God has given us.

It is similarly necessary to diminish the use of spices, which is one of the ships in which our gold is sent away from Germany. God's mercy has given us more food, and that both precious and good, than is to be found in other countries. I shall probably be accused of making foolish and impossible suggestions, as if I wished to destroy the great business of commerce. But I am only doing my part; if the community does not mend matters, every man should do it himself. I do not see many good manners that have ever come into a land through commerce, and therefore God let the people of Israel dwell far from the sea and not carry on much trade.

But without doubt the greatest misfortune of the Germans is buying on usury. But for this, many a man would have to leave unbought his silk, velvet, cloth of gold, spices, and all other luxuries. The system has not been in force for more than one hundred years, and has already brought poverty, misery, and destruction on almost all princes, foundations, cities, nobles, and heirs. If it continues for another hundred years Germany will be left without a farthing, and we shall be reduced to eating one another. The devil invented this system, and the Pope has done an injury to the whole world by sanctioning it.

My request and my cry therefore is this: Let each man consider the destruction of himself and his family, which is no longer at the door, but has entered the house; and let emperors, princes, lords, and corporations see to the condemnation and prohibition of this kind of trade, without considering the opposition of the Pope and all his justice and injustice, nor whether livings or endowments depend upon it. Better a single fief in a city based on a freehold estate or honest interest, than a hundred based on usury; yea, a single endowment on usury is worse and more grievous than twenty based on freehold estate. Truly this usury is a sign and warning that the world has been given over to the devil for its sins, and that we are losing our spiritual and temporal welfare alike; yet we heed it not.

Doubtless we should also find some bridle for the *Fuggers* and similar companies. Is it possible that in a single man's lifetime such great wealth should be collected together, if all were done rightly and according to God's will? I am not skilled in accounts, but I do not understand how it is possible for one hundred guilders to gain twenty in a year, or how one guilder can gain another, and that not out of the soil, or by cattle, seeing that possessions depend not on the wit of men, but on the blessing of God. I commend this to those that are skilled in worldly affairs. I as a theologian blame nothing but the evil appearance, of which St. Paul says, "Abstain from all appearance of evil" (I Thess. v. 22). All I know is that it were much more godly to encourage agriculture and lessen commerce; and that they do the best who, according to the Scriptures, till the ground to get their living, as we are all commanded in Adam: "Cursed is the ground for thy sake . . . Thorns also and thistles shall it bring forth to thee . . . In the sweat of thy face shalt thou eat bread" (Gen. iii. 17-19). There is still much ground that is not ploughed or tilled.

Then there is the excess in eating and drinking, for which we Germans have an ill reputation in foreign countries, as our special vice, and which has become so common, and gained so much the upper hand, that sermons avail nothing. The loss of money caused by it is not the worst; but in its train come murder, adultery, theft, blasphemy, and all vices. The temporal power should do something to prevent it; otherwise it will come to pass, as Christ foretold, that the last day shall come as a thief in the night, and shall find them eating and drinking, marrying and giving in marriage, planting and building, buying and selling (Matt. xxiv. 38; Luke xvii. 26), just as things go on now, and that so strongly that I apprehend lest the day of judgment be at hand, even now when we least expect it.

Lastly, is it not a terrible thing that we Christians should maintain public brothels, though we all vow chastity in our baptism? I well know all that can be said on this matter: that it is not peculiar to one nation, that it would be difficult to demolish it, and that it is better thus than that virgins, or married women, or honourable women should be dishonoured. But should not the spiritual and temporal powers combine to find some means of meeting this difficulties without any such heathen practice? If the people of Israel existed without this scandal, why should not a Christian nation be able to do so? How do so many towns and villages manage to exist without these houses? Why should not great cities be able to do so?

In all, however, that I have said above, my object has been to show how much good temporal authority might do, and what should be the duty of all authorities, so that every man might learn what a terrible thing it is to rule and to have the chief place. What boots it though a ruler be in his own person as holy as St. Peter, if he be not diligent to help his subjects in these matters? His very authority will be his condemnation; for it is the duty of those in authority to seek the good of their subjects. But if those in authority considered how young people might be brought together in marriage, the prospect of marriage would help every man and protect him from temptations.

But as it is every man is induced to become a priest or a monk; and of all these I am afraid not one in a hundred has any other motive but the wish of getting a livelihood and the uncertainty of maintaining a family. Therefore they begin by a dissolute life and sow their wild oats, (as they say), but I fear they rather gather in a store of wild oats.[39] I hold the proverb to be true, "Most men become monks and priests in desperation." That is why things are as we see them.

But in order that many sins may be prevented that are becoming too common, I would honestly advise that no boy or girl be allowed to take the vow of chastity or to enter a religious life before the age of thirty years. For this requires a special grace, as St. Paul says. Therefore, unless God specially urge any one to a

---

[39]Luther uses the expression *ausbuben* in the sense of *sich austoben,* viz., "to storm *out* one's passions," and then coins the word *sich einbuben,* viz., "to storm *in* one's passions."

religious life, he will do well to leave all vows and devotions alone. I say further, If a man has so little faith in God as to fear that he will be unable to maintain himself in the married state, and if this fear is the only thing that makes him become a priest, then I implore him, for his own soul's sake, not to become a priest, but rather to become a peasant, or what he will. For if simple trust in God be necessary to ensure temporal support, tenfold trust in God is necessary to live a religious life. If you do not trust to God for your worldly food, how can you trust to Him for your spiritual food? Alas! this unbelief and want of faith destroys all things, and leads us into all misery, as we see among all conditions of men.

Much might be said concerning all this misery. Young people have no one to look after them, they are left to go on just as they like, and those in authority are of no more use to them than if they did not exist, though this should be the chief care of the Pope, of bishops, lords, and councils. They wish to rule over everything, everywhere, and yet they are of no use. Oh, what a rare sight, for these reasons, will a lord or ruler be in heaven, though he might build a hundred churches to God and raise all the dead!

But this may suffice for the present. For of what concerns the temporal authority and the nobles I have, I think, said enough in my tract on *Good Works*. For their lives and governments leave room enough for improvement; but there is no comparison between spiritual and temporal abuses, as I have there shown. I daresay I have sung a lofty strain, that I have proposed many things that will be thought impossible, and attacked many points too sharply. But what was I to do? I was bound to say this: if I had the power, this is what I would do. I had rather incur the world's anger than God's; they cannot take from me more than my life. I have hitherto made many offers of peace to my adversaries; but, as I see, God has forced me through them to open my mouth wider and wider, and, because they do not keep quiet, to give them enough cause for speaking, barking, shouting, and writing. Well, then, I have another song still to sing concerning them and Rome; if they wish to hear it, I will sing it to them, and sing with all my might. Do you understand, my friend Rome, what I mean?

I have frequently offered to submit my writings for inquiry and examination, but in vain, though I know, if I am in the right, I must be condemned upon earth and justified by Christ alone in heaven. For all the Scriptures teach us that the affairs of Christians and Christendom must be judged by God alone; they have never yet been justified by men in this world, but the opposition has always been too strong. My greatest care and fear is lest my cause be not condemned by men, by which I should know for certain that it does not please God. Therefore let them go freely to work, pope, bishop, priest, monk, or doctor; they are the true people to persecute the truth, as they have always done. May God grant us all a Christian understanding, and especially to the Christian nobility of the German nation true spiritual courage, to do what is best for our unhappy Church. Amen!

At Wittenberg, in the year 1520.

CONCERNING
CHRISTIAN LIBERTY

LETTER OF MARTIN LUTHER TO POPE LEO X

AMONG those monstrous evils of this age with which I
have now for three years been waging war, I am sometimes compelled to look to you and to call you to mind,
most blessed father Leo. In truth, since you alone are everywhere considered as being the cause of my engaging in war, I
cannot at any time fail to remember you; and although I have
been compelled by the causeless raging of your impious flatterers against me to appeal from your seat to a future council—fearless of the futile decrees of your predecessors Pius and
Julius, who in their foolish tyranny prohibited such an
action—yet I have never been so alienated in feeling from your
Blessedness as not to have sought with all my might, in diligent
prayer and crying to God, all the best gifts for you and for your
see. But those who have hitherto endeavoured to terrify me with
the majesty of your name and authority, I have begun quite to
despise and triumph over. One thing I see remaining which I
cannot despise, and this has been the reason of my writing anew
to your Blessedness: namely, that I find that blame is cast on me,
and that it is imputed to me as a great offence, that in my rashness I am judged to have spared not even your person.

Now, to confess the truth openly, I am conscious that, whenever I have had to mention your person, I have said nothing of
you but what was honourable and good. If I had done otherwise, I could by no means have approved my own conduct, but
should have supported with all my power the judgment of those
men concerning me, nor would anything have pleased me better,
than to recant such rashness and impiety. I have called you
Daniel in Babylon; and every reader thoroughly knows with
what distinguished zeal I defended your conspicuous innocence
against Silvester, who tried to stain it. Indeed, the published

opinion of so many great men and the repute of your blameless life are too widely famed and too much reverenced throughout the world to be assailable by any man, of however great name, or by any arts. I am not so foolish as to attack one whom everybody praises; nay, it has been and always will be my desire not to attack even those whom public repute disgraces. I am not delighted at the faults of any man, since I am very conscious myself of the great beam in my own eye, nor can I be the first to cast a stone at the adulteress.

I have indeed inveighed sharply against impious doctrines, and I have not been slack to censure my adversaries on account, not of their bad morals, but of their impiety. And for this I am so far from being sorry that I have brought my mind to despise the judgments of men and to persevere in this vehement zeal, according to the example of Christ, who, in His zeal, calls His adversaries a generation of vipers, blind, hypocrites, and children of the devil. Paul, too, charges the sorcerer with being a child of the devil, full of all subtlety and all malice; and defames certain persons as evil workers, dogs, and deceivers. In the opinion of those delicate-eared persons, nothing could be more bitter or intemperate than Paul's language. What can be more bitter than the words of the prophets? The ears of our generation have been made so delicate by the senseless multitude of flatterers that, as soon as we perceive that anything of ours is not approved of, we cry out that we are being bitterly assailed; and when we can repel the truth by no other pretence, we escape by attributing bitterness, impatience, intemperance, to our adversaries. What would be the use of salt if it were not pungent, or of the edge of the sword if it did not slay? Accursed is the man who does the work of the Lord deceitfully.

Wherefore, most excellent Leo, I beseech you to accept my vindication, made in this letter, and to persuade yourself that I have never thought any evil concerning your person; further, that I am one who desires that eternal blessing may fall to your lot, and that I have no dispute with any man concerning morals, but only concerning the word of truth. In all other things I will yield to any one, but I neither can nor will forsake and deny the word. He who thinks otherwise of me, or has taken in my words in another sense, does not think rightly, and has not taken in the truth.

Your see, however, which is called the Court of Rome, and which neither you nor any man can deny to be more corrupt than any Babylon or Sodom, and quite, as I believe, of a lost, desperate, and hopeless impiety, this I have verily abominated, and have felt indignant that the people of Christ should be cheated under your name and the pretext of the Church of Rome; and so I have resisted, and will resist, as long as the spirit of faith shall live in me. Not that I am striving after impossibilities, or hoping that by my labours alone, against the furious opposition of so many flatterers, any good can be done in that most disordered Babylon; but that I feel myself a debtor to my brethren, and am bound to take thought for them, that fewer of them may be ruined, or that their ruin may be less complete, by the plagues of Rome. For many years now, nothing else has overflowed from Rome into the world—as you are not ignorant—than the laying waste of goods, of bodies, and of souls, and the worst examples of all the worst things. These things are clearer than the light to all men; and the Church of Rome, formerly the most holy of all Churches, has become the most lawless den of thieves, the most shameless of all brothels, the very kingdom of sin, death, and hell; so that not even antichrist, if he were to come, could devise any addition to its wickedness.

Meanwhile you, Leo, are sitting like a lamb in the midst of wolves, like Daniel in the midst of lions, and, with Ezekiel, you dwell among scorpions. What opposition can you alone make to these monstrous evils? Take to yourself three or four of the most learned and best of the cardinals. What are these among so many? You would all perish by poison before you could undertake to decide on a remedy. It is all over with the Court of Rome; the wrath of God has come upon her to the uttermost. She hates councils; she dreads to be reformed; she cannot restrain the madness of her impiety; she fills up the sentence passed on her mother, of whom it is said, "We would have healed Babylon, but she is not healed; let us forsake her." It had been your duty and that of your cardinals to apply a remedy to these evils, but this gout laughs at the physician's hand, and the chariot does not obey the reins. Under the influence of these feelings, I have always grieved that you, most excellent Leo, who were worthy of a better age, have been made pontiff in this. For the Roman Court is not worthy of you and those like you, but of Satan himself, who in truth is more the ruler in that Babylon than you are.

Oh, would that, having laid aside that glory which your most abandoned enemies declare to be yours, you were living rather in the office of a private priest or on your paternal inheritance! In that glory none are worthy to glory, except the race of Iscariot, the children of perdition. For what happens in your court, Leo, except that, the more wicked and execrable any man is, the more prosperously he can use your name and authority for the ruin of the property and souls of men, for the multiplication of crimes, for the oppression of faith and truth and of the whole Church of God? Oh, Leo! in reality most unfortunate, and sitting on a most perilous throne, I tell you the truth, because I wish you well; for if Bernard felt compassion for his Anastasius at a time when the Roman see, though even then most corrupt, was as yet ruling with better hope than now, why should not we lament, to whom so much further corruption and ruin has been added in three hundred years?

Is it not true that there is nothing under the vast heavens more corrupt, more pestilential, more hateful, than the Court of Rome? She incomparably surpasses the impiety of the Turks, so that in very truth she, who was formerly the gate of heaven, is now a sort of open mouth of hell, and such a mouth as, under the urgent wrath of God, cannot be blocked up; one course alone being left to us wretched men: to call back and save some few, if we can, from that Roman gulf.

Behold, Leo, my father, with what purpose and on what principle it is that I have stormed against that seat of pestilence. I am so far from having felt any rage against your person that I even hoped to gain favour with you and to aid you in your welfare by striking actively and vigorously at that your prison, nay, your hell. For whatever the efforts of all minds can contrive against the confusion of that impious Court will be advantageous to you and to your welfare, and to many others with you. Those who do harm to her are doing your office; those who in every way abhor her are glorifying Christ; in short, those are Christians who are not Romans.

But, to say yet more, even this never entered my heart: to inveigh against the Court of Rome or to dispute at all about her. For, seeing all remedies for her health to be desperate, I looked on her with contempt, and, giving her a bill of divorcement, said to her, "He that is unjust, let him be unjust still; and he that is filthy, let him be filthy still," giving myself up to the peaceful and quiet study of sacred literature, that by this I might be of use to the brethren living about me.

While I was making some advance in these studies, Satan opened his eyes and goaded on his servant John Eccius, that notorious adversary of Christ, by the unchecked lust for fame, to drag me unexpectedly into the arena, trying to catch me in one little word concerning the primacy of the Church of Rome, which had fallen from me in passing. That boastful Thraso, foaming and gnashing his teeth, proclaimed that he would dare all things for the glory of God and for the honour of the holy apostolic seat; and, being puffed up respecting your power, which he was about to misuse, he looked forward with all certainty to victory; seeking to promote, not so much the primacy of Peter, as his own pre-eminence among the theologians of this age; for he thought it would contribute in no slight degree to this, if he were to lead Luther in triumph. The result having proved unfortunate for the sophist, an incredible rage torments him; for he feels that whatever discredit to Rome has arisen through me has been caused by the fault of himself alone.

Suffer me, I pray you, most excellent Leo, both to plead my own cause, and to accuse your true enemies. I believe it is known to you in what way Cardinal Cajetan, your imprudent and unfortunate, nay unfaithful, legate, acted towards me. When, on account of my reverence for your name, I had placed myself and all that was mine in his hands, he did not so act as to establish peace, which he could easily have established by one little word, since I, at that time, promised to be silent and to make an end of my case, if he would command my adversaries to do the same. But that man of pride, not content with this agreement, began to justify my adversaries, to give them free licence, and to order me to recant, a thing which was certainly not in his commission. Thus indeed, when the case was in the best position, it came through his vexatious tyranny into a much worse one. Therefore, whatever has followed upon this is the fault not of Luther, but entirely of Cajetan, since he did not suffer me to be silent and remain quiet, which at that time I was entreating for with all my might. What more was it my duty to do?

Next came Charles Miltitz, also a nuncio from your Blessedness. He, though he went up and down with much and varied exertion, and omitted nothing which could tend to restore the position of the cause thrown into confusion by the rashness and pride of Cajetan, had difficulty, even with the help of that very illustrious prince the Elector Frederick, in at last bringing about more than one familiar conference with me. In these I again yielded to your great name, and was prepared to keep silence, and to accept as my judge either the Archbishop of Treves, or the Bishop of Naumburg; and thus it was done and concluded. While this was being done with good hope of success, lo! that other and greater enemy of yours, Eccius, rushed in with his Leipsic disputation, which he had undertaken against Carlstadt, and, having taken up a new question concerning the primacy of the Pope, turned his arms unexpectedly against me, and completely overthrew the plan for peace. Meanwhile Charles Miltitz was waiting, disputations were held, judges were being chosen, but no decision was arrived at. And no wonder! for by the falsehoods, pretences, and arts of Eccius the whole business was brought into such thorough disorder, confusion, and festering soreness, that, whichever way the sentence might lean, a greater conflagration was sure to arise; for he was seeking, not after truth, but after his own credit. In this case too, I omitted nothing which it was right that I should do.

I confess that on this occasion no small part of the corruptions of Rome came to light; but, if there was any offence in this, it was the fault of Eccius, who, in taking on him a burden beyond his strength, and in furiously aiming at credit for himself, unveiled to the whole world the disgrace of Rome.

Here is that enemy of yours, Leo, or rather of your Court; by his example alone we may learn that an enemy is not more baneful than a flatterer. For what did he bring about by his flattery, except evils which no king could have brought about? At this day, the name of the Court of Rome stinks in the nostrils of the world, the papal authority is growing weak, and its notorious ignorance is evil spoken of. We should hear none of these things, if Eccius had not disturbed the plans of Miltitz and myself for peace. He feels this clearly enough himself in the indignation he shows, too late and in vain, against the publication of my books. He ought to have reflected on this at the time when he was all mad for renown, and was seeking in your cause nothing but his own objects, and that with the greatest peril to you. The foolish man hoped that, from fear of your name, I should yield and keep silence; for I do not think he presumed on his talents and learning. Now, when he sees that I am very confident and speak aloud, he repents too late of his rashness, and sees—if indeed he does see it—that there is One in heaven who resists the proud, and humbles the presumptuous.

Since then we were bringing about by this disputation nothing but the greater confusion of the cause of Rome, Charles Miltitz for the third time addressed the Fathers of the Order, assembled in chapter, and sought their advice for the settlement of the case, as being now in a most troubled and perilous state. Since, by the favour of God, there was no hope of proceeding against me by force, some of the more noted of their number were sent to me, and begged me at least to show respect to your person and to vindicate in a humble letter both your innocence and my own. They said that the affair was not as yet in a position of extreme hopelessness, if Leo X., in his inborn kindliness, would put his hand to it. On this I, who have always offered and wished for peace, in order that I might devote myself to calmer and more useful pursuits, and who for this very purpose have acted with so much spirit and vehemence, in order to put down by the strength and impetuosity of my words, as well as of my feelings, men whom I saw to be very far from equal to myself—I, I say, not only gladly yielded, but even accepted it with joy and gratitude, as the greatest kindness and benefit, if you should think it right to satisfy my hopes.

Thus I come, most blessed Father, and in all abasement beseech you to put your hand, if it is possible, and impose a curb to those flatterers who are enemies of peace, while they pretend peace. But there is no reason, most blessed Father, why any one should assume that I am to utter a recantation, unless he prefers to involve the case in still greater confusion. Moreover, I cannot bear with laws for the interpretation of the word of God, since the word of God, which teaches liberty in all other things, ought not to be bound. Saving these two things, there is nothing which I am not able, and most heartily willing, to do or to suffer. I hate contention; I will challenge no one; in return I wish not to be challenged; but, being challenged, I will not be dumb in the cause of Christ, my Master. For your Blessedness will be able by one short and easy word to call these controversies before you and suppress them, and to impose silence and peace on both sides—a word which I have ever longed to hear.

Therefore, Leo, my Father, beware of listening to those sirens who make you out to be not simply a man, but partly a god, so that you can command and require whatever you will. It will not happen so, nor will you prevail. You are the servant of servants, and more than any other man, in a most pitiable and perilous position. Let not those men deceive you who pretend that you are lord of the world; who will not allow any one to be a Christian without your authority; who babble of your having power over heaven, hell, and purgatory. These men are your enemies and are seeking your soul to destroy it, as Isaiah says, "My people they that call thee blessed are themselves deceiving thee." They are in error who raise you above councils and the universal Church; they are in error who attribute to you alone the right of interpreting Scripture. All these men are seeking to set up their own impieties in the Church under your name, and alas! Satan has gained much through them in the time of your predecessors.

In brief, trust not in any who exalt you, but in those who humiliate you. For this is the judgment of God: "He hath cast down the mighty from their seat, and hath exalted the humble." See how unlike Christ was to His successors, though all will have it that they are His vicars. I fear that in truth very many of them have been in too serious a sense His vicars, for a vicar represents a prince who is absent. Now if a pontiff rules while Christ is absent and does not dwell in his heart, what else is he but a vicar of Christ? And then what is that Church but a multitude without Christ? What indeed is such a vicar but antichrist and an idol? How much more rightly did the Apostles speak, who call themselves servants of a present Christ, not the vicars of an absent one!

Perhaps I am shamelessly bold in seeming to teach so great a head, by whom all men ought to be taught, and from whom, as those plagues of yours boast, the thrones of judges receive their sentence; but I imitate St. Bernard in his book concerning *Considerations* addressed to Eugenius, a book which ought to be known by heart by every pontiff. I do this, not from any desire to teach, but as a duty, from that simple and faithful solicitude which teaches us to be anxious for all that is safe for our neighbours, and does not allow considerations of worthiness or unworthiness to be entertained, being intent only on the dangers or advantage of others. For since I know that your Blessedness is driven and tossed by the waves at Rome, so that the depths of the sea press on you with infinite perils, and that you are labouring under such a condition of misery that you need even the least help from any the least brother, I do not seem to myself to be

acting unsuitably if I forget your majesty till I shall have fulfilled the office of charity. I will not flatter in so serious and
perilous a matter; and if in this you do not see that I am your
friend and most thoroughly your subject, there is One to see and
judge.

In fine, that I may not approach you empty-handed, blessed
Father, I bring with me this little treatise, published under your
name, as a good omen of the establishment of peace and of good
hope. By this you may perceive in what pursuits I should prefer
and be able to occupy myself to more profit, if I were allowed,
or had been hitherto allowed, by your impious flatterers. It is a
small matter, if you look to its exterior, but, unless I mistake, it
is a summary of the Christian life put together in small compass,
if you apprehend its meaning. I, in my poverty, have no other
present to make you, nor do you need anything else than to be
enriched by a spiritual gift. I commend myself to your Paternity
and Blessedness, whom may the Lord Jesus preserve for ever.
Amen.

Wittenberg, 6th September, 1520.

CONCERNING CHRISTIAN LIBERTY

Christian faith has appeared to many an easy thing; nay, not a
few even reckon it among the social virtues, as it were; and this
they do because they have not made proof of it experimentally,
and have never tasted of what efficacy it is. For it is not possible
for any man to write well about it, or to understand well what is
rightly written, who has not at some time tasted of its spirit,
under the pressure of tribulation; while he who has tasted of it,
even to a very small extent, can never write, speak, think, or
hear about it sufficiently. For it is a living fountain, springing up
into eternal life, as Christ calls it in John iv.

Now, though I cannot boast of my abundance, and though I
know how poorly I am furnished, yet I hope that, after having

been vexed by various temptations, I have attained some little drop of faith, and that I can speak of this matter, if not with more elegance, certainly with more solidity, than those literal and too subtle disputants who have hitherto discoursed upon it without understanding their own words. That I may open then an easier way for the ignorant—for these alone I am trying to serve—I first lay down these two propositions, concerning spiritual liberty and servitude:—

A Christian man is the most free lord of all, and subject to none; a Christian man is the most dutiful servant of all, and subject to every one.

Although these statements appear contradictory, yet, when they are found to agree together, they will do excellently for my purpose. They are both the statements of Paul himself, who says, "Though I be free from all men, yet have I made myself servant unto all" (I Cor. ix. 19), and "Owe no man anything, but to love one another" (Rom. xiii. 8). Now love is by its own nature dutiful and obedient to the beloved object. Thus even Christ, though Lord of all things, was yet made of a woman; made under the law; at once free and a servant; at once in the form of God and in the form of a servant.

Let us examine the subject on a deeper and less simple principle. Man is composed of a twofold nature, a spiritual and a bodily. As regards the spiritual nature, which they name the soul, he is called the spiritual, inward, new man; as regards the bodily nature, which they name the flesh, he is called the fleshly, outward, old man. The Apostle speaks of this: "Though our outward man perish, yet the inward man is renewed day by day" (2 Cor. iv. 16). The result of this diversity is that in the Scriptures opposing statements are made concerning the same man, the fact being that in the same man these two men are opposed to one another; the flesh lusting against the spirit, and the spirit against the flesh (Gal. v. 17).

We first approach the subject of the inward man, that we may see by what means a man becomes justified, free, and a true Christian; that is, a spiritual, new, and inward man. It is certain that absolutely none among outward things, under whatever name they may be reckoned, has any influence in producing Christian righteousness or liberty, nor, on the other hand, unrighteousness or slavery. This can be shown by an easy argument.

What can it profit the soul that the body should be in good condition, free, and full of life; that it should eat, drink, and act according to its pleasure; when even the most impious slaves of every kind of vice are prosperous in these matters? Again, what harm can ill-health, bondage, hunger, thirst, or any other outward evil, do to the soul, when even the most pious of men and the freest in the purity of their conscience, are harassed by these things? Neither of these states of things has to do with the liberty or the slavery of the soul.

And so it will profit nothing that the body should be adorned with sacred vestments, or dwell in holy places, or be occupied in sacred offices, or pray, fast, and abstain from certain meats, or do whatever works can be done through the body and in the body. Something widely different will be necessary for the justification and liberty of the soul, since the things I have spoken of can be done by any impious person, and only hypocrites are produced by devotion to these things. On the other hand, it will not at all injure the soul that the body should be clothed in profane raiment, should dwell in profane places, should eat and drink in the ordinary fashion, should not pray aloud, and should leave undone all the things above mentioned, which may be done by hypocrites.

And, to cast everything aside, even speculation, meditations, and whatever things can be performed by the exertions of the soul itself, are of no profit. One thing, and one alone, is necessary for life, justification, and Christian liberty; and that is the most holy word of God, the Gospel of Christ, as He says, "I am the resurrection and the life; he that believeth in Me shall not die eternally" (John xi. 25), and also, "If the Son shall make you free, ye shall be free indeed" (John viii. 36), and "Man shall not live by bread alone, but by every word that proceedeth out of the mouth of God'' (Matt. iv. 4).

Let us therefore hold it for certain and firmly established that the soul can do without everything except the word of God, without which none at all of its wants are provided for. But, having the word, it is rich and wants for nothing, since that is the word of life, of truth, of light, of peace, of justification, of salvation, of joy, of liberty, of wisdom, of virtue, of grace, of glory, and of every good thing. It is on this account that the prophet in a whole Psalm (Psalm cxix.) and in many other places, sighs for and calls upon the word of God with so many groanings and words.

Again, there is no more cruel stroke of the wrath of God than when He sends a famine of hearing His words (Amos viii. 11), just as there is no greater favour from Him than the sending forth of His word, as it is said, ''He sent His word and healed them, and delivered them from their destructions'' (Psalm cvii. 20). Christ was sent for no other office than that of the word; and the order of Apostles, that of bishops, and that of the whole body of the clergy, have been called and instituted for no object but the ministry of the word.

But you will ask, What is this word, and by what means is it to be used, since there are so many words of God? I answer, The Apostle Paul (Rom. i.) explains what it is, namely the Gospel of God, concerning His Son, incarnate, suffering, risen, and glorified, through the Spirit, the Sanctifier. To preach Christ is to feed the soul, to justify it, to set it free, and to save it, if it believes the preaching. For faith alone and the efficacious use of the word of God, bring salvation. ''If thou shalt confess with thy mouth the Lord Jesus, and shalt believe in thine heart that God hath raised Him from the dead, thou shalt be saved'' (Rom. x. 9); and again, ''Christ is the end of the law for righteousness to every one that believeth'' (Rom. x. 4), and ''The just shall live by faith'' (Rom. i. 17). For the word of God cannot be received and honoured by any works, but by faith alone. Hence it is clear that as the soul needs the word alone for life and justification, so it is justified by faith alone, and not by any works. For if it could be justified by any other means, it would have no need of the word, nor consequently of faith.

But this faith cannot consist at all with works; that is, if you imagine that you can be justified by those works, whatever they are, along with it. For this would be to halt between two opinions, to worship Baal, and to kiss the hand to him, which is a very great iniquity, as Job says. Therefore, when you begin to believe, you learn at the same time that all that is in you is utterly guilty, sinful, and damnable, according to that saying, "All have sinned, and come short of the glory of God" (Rom. iii. 23), and also: "There is none righteous, no, not one; they are all gone out of the way; they are together become unprofitable: there is none that doeth good, no, not one" (Rom. iii. 10-12). When you have learnt this, you will know that Christ is necessary for you, since He has suffered and risen again for you, that, believing on Him, you might by this faith become another man, all your sins being remitted, and you being justified by the merits of another, namely of Christ alone.

Since then this faith can reign only in the inward man, as it is said, "With the heart man believeth unto righteousness" (Rom. x. 10); and since it alone justifies, it is evident that by no outward work or labour can the inward man be at all justified, made free, and saved; and that no works whatever have any relation to him. And so, on the other hand, it is solely by impiety and incredulity of heart that he becomes guilty and a slave of sin, deserving condemnation, not by any outwad sin or work. Therefore, the first care of every Christian ought to be to lay aside all reliance on works, and strengthen his faith alone more and more, and by it grow in the knowledge, not of works, but of Christ Jesus, who has suffered and risen again for him, as Peter teaches (I Peter v.) when he makes no other work to be a Christian one. Thus Christ, when the Jews asked Him what they should do that they might work the works of God, rejected the multitude of works, with which He saw that they were puffed up, and commanded them one thing only, saying, "This is the work of God: that ye believe on Him whom He hath sent, for

Him hath God the Father sealed'' (John vi. 27, 29).

Hence a right faith in Christ is an incomparable treasure, carrying with it universal salvation and preserving from all evil, as it is said, ''He that believeth and is baptised shall be saved; but he that believeth not shall be damned'' (Mark xvi. 16). Isaiah, looking to this treasure, predicted, ''The consumption decreed shall overflow with righteousness. For the Lord God of hosts shall make a consumption, even determined (*verbum abbreviatum et consummans*), in the midst of the land'' (Isa. x. 22, 23). As if he said, ''Faith, which is the brief and complete fulfilling of the law, will fill those who believe with such righteousness that they will need nothing else for justification.'' Thus, too, Paul says, ''For with the heart man believeth unto righteousness'' (Rom. x. 10).

But you ask how it can be the fact that faith alone justifies, and affords without works so great a treasure of good things, when so many works, ceremonies, and laws are prescribed to us in the Scriptures? I answer: Before all things bear in mind what I have said: that faith alone without works justifies, sets free, and saves, as I shall show more clearly below.

Meanwhile it is to be noted that the whole Scripture of God is divided into two parts: precepts and promises. The precepts certainly teach us what is good, but what they teach is not forthwith done. For they show us what we ought to do, but do not give us the power to do it. They were ordained, however, for the purpose of showing man to himself, that through them he may learn his own impotence for good and may despair of his own strength. For this reason they are called the Old Testament, and are so.

For example, ''Thou shalt not covet,'' is a precept by which we are all convicted of sin, since no man can help coveting, whatever efforts to the contrary he may make. In order therefore that he may fulfil the precept, and not covet, he is constrained to despair of himself and to seek elsewhere and through another the help which he cannot find in himself; as it is said, ''O Israel, thou hast destroyed thyself; but in Me is thine help''

(Hosea xiii. 9). Now what is done by this one precept is done by all; for all are equally impossible of fulfilment by us.

Now when a man has through the precepts been taught his own impotence, and become anxious by what means he may satisfy the law—for the law must be satisfied, so that no jot or tittle of it may pass away, otherwise he must be hopelessly condemned—then, being truly humbled and brought to nothing in his own eyes, he finds in himself no resource for justification and salvation.

Then comes in that other part of Scripture, the promises of God, which declare the glory of God, and say, "If you wish to fulfil the law, and, as the law requires, not to covet, lo! believe in Christ, in whom are promised to you grace, justification, peace and liberty." All these things you shall have, if you believe, and shall be without them if you do not believe. For what is impossible for you by all the works of the law, which are many and yet useless, you shall fulfil in an easy and summary way through faith, because God the Father has made everything to depend on faith, so that whosoever has it has all things, and he who has it not has nothing. "For God hath concluded them all in unbelief, that He might have mercy upon all" (Rom. xi. 32). Thus the promises of God give that which the precepts exact, and fulfil what the law commands; so that all is of God alone, both the precepts and their fulfilment. He alone commands; He alone also fulfils. Hence the promises of God belong to the New Testament; nay, are the New Testament.

Now, since these promises of God are words of holiness, truth, righteousness, liberty, and peace, and are full of universal goodness, the soul, which cleaves to them with a firm faith, is so united to them, nay thoroughly absorbed by them, that it not only partakes in, but is penetrated and saturated by, all their virtues. For if the touch of Christ was healing, how much more does that most tender spiritual touch, nay, absorption of the word, communicate to the soul all that belongs to the word! In this way therefore the soul, through faith alone, without works, is from the word of God justified, sanctified, endued with truth, peace, and liberty, and filled full with every good thing, and is truly made the child of God, as it is said, "To them gave He power to become the sons of God, even to them that believe on His name" (John i. 12).

From all this it is easy to understand why faith has such great power, and why no good works, nor even all good works put together, can compare with it, since no work can cleave to the word of God or be in the soul. Faith alone and the word reign in it; and such as is the word, such is the soul made by it, just as iron exposed to fire glows like fire, on account of its union with the fire. It is clear then that to a Christian man his faith suffices for everything, and that he has no need of works for justification. But if he has no need of works, neither has he need of the law; and if he has no need of the law, he is certainly free from the law, and the saying is true, "The law is not made for a righteous man" (I Tim. i. 9). This is that Christian liberty, our faith, the effect of which is, not that we should be careless or lead a bad life, but that no one should need the law or works for justification and salvation.

Let us consider this as the first virtue of faith; and let us look also to the second. This also is an office of faith: that it honours with the utmost veneration and the highest reputation Him in whom it believes, inasmuch as it holds Him to be truthful and worthy of belief. For there is no honour like that reputation of truth and righteousness with which we honour Him in whom we believe. What higher credit can we attribute to any one than truth and righteousness, and absolute goodness? On the other hand, it is the greatest insult to brand any one with the reputation of falsehood and unrighteousness, or to suspect him of these, as we do when we disbelieve him.

Thus the soul, in firmly believing the promises of God, holds Him to be true and righteous; and it can attribute to God no higher glory than the credit of being so. The highest worship of God is to ascribe to Him, truth, righteousness, and whatever qualities we must ascribe to one in whom we believe. In doing this, the soul shows itself prepared to do His whole will; in doing this it hallows His name, and gives itself up to be dealt with as it may please God. For it cleaves to His promises, and never doubts that He is true, just, and wise, and will do, dispose, and provide for all things in the best way. Is not such a soul, in this its faith, most obedient to God in all things? What commandment does there remain which has not been amply fulfilled by such an obedience? What fulfilment can be more full than universal obedience? Now this is not accomplished by works, but by faith alone.

On the other hand, what greater rebellion, impiety, or insult to God can there be, than not to believe His promises? What else is this, than either to make God a liar, or to doubt His truth—that is, to attribute truth to ourselves, but to God falsehood and levity? In doing this, is not a man denying God and setting himself up as an idol in his own heart? What then can works, done in such a state of impiety, profit us, were they even angelic or apostolic works? Rightly hath God shut up all, not in wrath nor in lust, but in unbelief, in order that those who pretend that they are fulfilling the law by works of purity and benevolence (which are social and human virtues) may not presume that they will therefore be saved, but, being included in the sin of unbelief, may either seek mercy, or be justly condemned.

But when God sees that truth is ascribed to Him, and that in the faith of our hearts He is honoured with all the honour of which He is worthy, then in return He honours us on account of that faith, attributing to us truth and righteousness. For faith does truth and righteousness in rendering to God what is His; and therefore in return, God gives glory to our righteousness. It is true and righteous that God is true and righteous; and to confess this and ascribe these attributes to Him, this it is to be true and righteous. Thus He says, "Them that honour Me I will honour, and they that despise Me shall be lightly esteemed" (I Sam. ii. 30). And so Paul says that Abraham's faith was imputed to him for righteousness, because by it he gave glory to God; and that to us also, for the same reason, it shall be imputed for righteousness, if we believe (Rom. iv.).

The third incomparable grace of faith is this: that it unites the soul to Christ, as the wife to the husband, by which mystery, as the Apostle teaches, Christ and the soul are made one flesh. Now if they are one flesh, and if a true marriage—nay, by far the most perfect of all marriages—is accomplished between them (for human marriages are but feeble types of this one great marriage), then it follows that all they have becomes theirs in common, as well good things as evil things; so that whatsoever Christ possesses, that the believing soul may take to itself and boast of as its own, and whatever belongs to the soul, that Christ claims as His.

If we compare these possessions, we shall see how inestimable is the gain. Christ is full of grace, life, and salvation; the soul is full of sin, death, and condemnation. Let faith step in, and then sin, death, and hell will belong to Christ, and grace, life, and salvation to the soul. For, if He is a Husband, He must needs take to Himself that which is His wife's and at the same time, impart to His wife that which is His. For, in giving her His own body and Himself, how can He but give her all that is His? And, in taking to Himself the body of His wife, how can He but take to Himself all that is hers?

In this is displayed the delightful sight, not only of communion, but of a prosperous warfare, of victory, salvation, and redemption. For, since Christ is God and man, and is such a Person as neither has sinned, nor dies, nor is condemned, nay, cannot sin, die, or be condemned, and since His righteousness, life, and salvation are invincible, eternal, and almighty,—when I say, such a Person, by the wedding-ring of faith, takes a share in the sins, death, and hell of His wife, nay, makes them His own, and deals with them no otherwise than as if they were His, and as if He Himself had sinned; and when He suffers, dies, and descends to hell, that He may overcome all things, and since sin, death, and hell cannot swallow Him up, they must needs be swallowed up by Him in stupendous conflict. For His righeousness rises above the sins of all men; His life is more powerful than all death; His salvation is more unconquerable than all hell.

Thus the believing soul, by the pledge of its faith in Christ, becomes free from all sin, fearless of death, safe from hell, and endowed with the eternal righteousness, life, and salvation of its Husband Christ. Thus He presents to Himself a glorious bride, without spot or wrinkle, cleansing her with the washing of water by the word; that is, by faith in the word of life, righteousness, and salvation. Thus He betrothes her unto Himself "in faithfulness, in righteousness, and in judgment, and in loving kindness, and in mercies" (Hosea ii. 19, 20).

Who then can value highly enough these royal nuptials? Who can comprehend the riches of the glory of this grace? Christ, that rich and pious Husband, takes as a wife a needy and impious harlot, redeeming her from all her evils and supplying her with all His good things. It is impossible now that her sins should destroy her, since they have been laid upon Christ and swallowed up in Him, and since she has in her Husband Christ, a righteousness which she may claim as her own, and which she can set up with confidence against all her sins, against death and hell, saying, "If I have sinned, my Christ, in whom I believe, has not sinned; all mine is His, and all His is mine," as it is written, "My beloved is mine, and I am His" (Cant. ii. 16). This is what Paul says: "Thanks be to God, which giveth us the victory through our Lord Jesus Christ," victory over sin and death, as he says, "The sting of death is sin, and the strength of sin is the law" (I Cor. xv. 56, 57).

From all this you will again understand why so much importance is attributed to faith, so that it alone can fulfil the law and justify without any works. For you see that the First Commandment, which says, "Thou shalt worship one God only," is fulfilled by faith alone. If you were nothing but good works from the soles of your feet to the crown of your head, you would not be worshipping God, nor fulfilling the First Commandment, since it is impossible to worship God without ascribing to Him the glory of truth and of universal goodness, as it ought in truth to be ascribed. Now this is not done by works, but only by faith of heart. It is not by working, but by believing, that we glorify

God, and confess Him to be true. On this ground, faith alone is the righteousness of a Christian man, and the fulfilling of all the commandments. For to him who fulfils the first, the task of fulfilling all the rest is easy.

Works, since they are irrational things, cannot glorify God, although they may be done to the glory of God, if faith be present. But at present we are inquiring, not into the quality of the works done, but into him who does them, who glorifies God, and brings forth good works. This is faith of heart, the head and the substance of all our righteousness. Hence that is a blind and perilous doctrine which teaches that the commandments are fulfilled by works. The commandments must have been fulfilled previous to any good works, and good works follow their fulfillment, as we shall see.

But, that we may have a wider view of that grace which our inner man has in Christ, we must know that in the Old Testament, God sanctified to Himself every first-born male. The birthright was of great value, giving a superiority over the rest by the double honour of priesthood and kingship. For the first-born brother was priest and lord of all the rest.

Under this figure was foreshown Christ, the true and only First-born of God the Father and of the Virgin Mary, and a true King and Priest, not in a fleshly and earthly sense. For His kingdom is not of this world; it is in heavenly and spiritual things that He reigns and acts as Priest; and these are righteousness, truth, wisdom, peace, salvation, etc. Not but that all things, even those of earth and hell, are subject to Him—for otherwise how could He defend and save us from them?—but it is not in these, nor by these, that His kingdom stands.

So, too, His priesthood does not consist in the outward display of vestments and gestures, as did the human priesthood of Aaron and our ecclesiastical priesthood at this day, but in spiritual things, wherein, in His invisible office, He intercedes for us with God in heaven, and there offers Himself, and performs all the duties of a priest, as Paul describes Him to the Hebrews under the figure of Melchizedek. Nor does He only pray and intercede for us; He also teaches us inwardly in the spirit with the living teachings of His Spirit. Now these are the two special offices of a priest, as is figured to us in the case of fleshly priests by visible prayers and sermons.

As Christ by His birthright has obtained these two dignities, so He imparts and communicates them to every believer in Him, under that law of matrimony of which we have spoken above, by which all that is the husband's is also the wife's. Hence all we who believe on Christ are kings and priests in Christ, as it is said, "Ye are a chosen generation, a royal priesthood, a holy nation, a peculiar people, that ye should show forth the praises of Him who hath called you out of darkness into His marvellous light" (I Peter ii. 9).

These two things stand thus. First, as regards kingship, every Christian is by faith so exalted above all things that, in spiritual power, he is completely lord of all things, so that nothing whatever can do him any hurt; yea, all things are subject to him, and are compelled to be subservient to his salvation. Thus Paul says, "All things work together for good to them who are called" (Rom. viii. 28), and also, "Whether life, or death, or things present, or things to come, all are yours; and ye are Christ's" (I Cor. iii. 22, 23).

Not that in the sense of corporeal power any one among Christians has been appointed to possess and rule all things, according to the mad and senseless idea of certain ecclesiastics. That is the office of kings, princes, and men upon earth. In the experience of life we see that we are subjected to all things, and suffer many things, even death. Yea, the more of a Christian any man is, to so many the more evils, sufferings, and deaths is he subject, as we see in the first place in Christ the First-born, and in all His holy brethren.

This is a spiritual power, which rules in the midst of enemies, and is powerful in the midst of distresses. And this is nothing else than that strength is made perfect in my weakness, and that I can turn all things to the profit of my salvation; so that even the cross and death are compelled to serve me and to work together for my salvation. This is a lofty and eminent dignity, a true and almighty dominion, a spiritual empire, in which there is nothing so good, nothing so bad, as not to work together for my good, if only I believe. And yet there is nothing of which I have need—for faith alone suffices for my salvation—unless that in it faith may exercise the power and empire of its liberty. This is the inestimable power and liberty of Christians.

Nor are we only kings and the freest of all men, but also priests for ever, a dignity far higher than kingship, because by that priesthood we are worthy to appear before God, to pray for others, and to teach one another mutually the things which are of God. For these are the duties of priests, and they cannot possibly be permitted to any unbeliever. Christ has obtained for us this favour, if we believe in Him: that just as we are His brethren and co-heirs and fellow-kings with Him, so we should be also fellow-priests with Him, and venture with confidence, through the spirit of faith, to come into the presence of God, and cry, "Abba, Father!" and to pray for one another, and to do all things which we see done and figured in the visible and corporeal office of priesthood. But to an unbelieving person nothing renders service or work for good. He himself is in servitude to all things, and all things turn out for evil to him, because he uses all things in an impious way for his own advantage, and not for the glory of God. And thus he is not a priest, but a profane person, whose prayers are turned into sin, nor does he ever appear in the presence of God, because God does not hear sinners.

Who then can comprehend the loftiness of that Christian dignity which, by its royal power, rules over all things, even over death, life, and sin, and, by its priestly glory, is all-powerful with God, since God does what He Himself seeks and wishes, as it is written, "He will fulfil the desire of them that fear Him; He also will hear their cry, and will save them"? (Psalm cxlv. 19). This glory certainly cannot be attained by any works, but by faith only.

From these considerations any one may clearly see how a Christian man is free from all things; so that he needs no works in order to be justified and saved, but receives these gifts in abundance from faith alone. Nay, were he so foolish as to pretend to be justified, set free, saved, and made a Christian, by means of any good work, he would immediately lose faith, with all its benefits. Such folly is prettily represented in the fable where a dog, running along in the water and carrying in his mouth a real piece of meat, is deceived by the reflection of the meat in the water, and, in trying with open mouth to seize it, loses the meat and its image at the same time.

Here you will ask, "If all who are in the Church are priests, by what character are those whom we now call priests to be distinguished from the laity?" I reply, By the use of these words, "priest," "clergy," "spiritual person," "ecclesiastic," an injustice has been done, since they have been transferred from the remaining body of Christians to those few who are now, by hurtful custom, called ecclesiastics. For Holy Scripture makes no distinction between them, except that those who are now boastfully called popes, bishops, and lords, it calls ministers, servants, and stewards, who are to serve the rest in the ministry of the word, for teaching the faith of Christ and the liberty of believers. For though it is true that we are all equally priests, yet we cannot, nor, if we could, ought we all to, minister and teach publicly. Thus Paul says, "Let a man so account of us as of the ministers of Christ and stewards of the mysteries of God" (I Cor. iv. 1).

This bad system has now issued in such a pompous display of power and such a terrible tyranny that no earthly government can be compared to it, as if the laity were something else than Christians. Through this perversion of things it has happened that the knowledge of Christian grace, of faith, of liberty, and altogether of Christ, has utterly perished, and has been succeeded by an intolerable bondage to human works and laws; and, according to the Lamentations of Jeremiah, we have become the slaves of the vilest men on earth, who abuse our misery to all the disgraceful and ignominious purposes of their own will.

Returning to the subject which we had begun, I think it is made clear by these considerations that it is not sufficient, nor a Christian course, to preach the works, life, and words of Christ in a historic manner, as facts which it suffices to know as an example how to frame our life, as do those who are now held the best preachers, and much less so to keep silence altogether on these things and to teach in their stead the laws of men and the decrees of the Fathers. There are now not a few persons who preach and read about Christ with the object of moving the human affections to sympathize with Christ, to indignation against the Jews, and other childish and womanish absurdities of that kind.

Now preaching ought to have the object of promoting faith in Him, so that He may not only be Christ, but a Christ for you and for me, and that what is said of Him, and what He is called, may work in us. And this faith is produced and is maintained by preaching why Christ came, what He has brought us and given to us, and to what profit and advantage He is to be received. This is done when the Christian liberty which we have from Christ Himself is rightly taught, and we are shown in what manner all we Christians are kings and priests, and how we are lords of all things, and may be confident that whatever we do in the presence of God is pleasing and acceptable to Him.

Whose heart would not rejoice in its inmost core at hearing these things? Whose heart, on receiving so great a consolation, would not become sweet with the love of Christ, a love to which it can never attain by any laws or works? Who can injure such a heart, or make it afraid? If the consciousness of sin or the horror of death rush in upon it, it is prepared to hope in the Lord, and is fearless of such evils, and undisturbed, until it shall look down upon its enemies. For it believes that the righteousness of Christ is its own, and that its sin is no longer its own, but that of Christ; but, on account of its faith in Christ, all its sin must needs be swallowed up from before the face of the righteousness of Christ, as I have said above. It learns, too, with the Apostle, to scoff at death and sin, and to say, ''O death, where is thy sting?

O grave, where is thy victory? The sting of death is sin, and the strength of sin is the law. But thanks be to God, which giveth us the victory through our Lord Jesus Christ'' (I Cor. xv. 55-57). For death is swallowed up in victory, not only the victory of Christ, but ours also, since by faith it becomes ours, and in it we too conquer.

Let it suffice to say this concerning the inner man and its liberty, and concerning that righteousness of faith which needs neither laws nor good works; nay, they are even hurtful to it, if any one pretends to be justified by them.

And now let us turn to the other part: to the outward man. Here we shall give an answer to all those who, taking offence at the word of faith and at what I have asserted, say, ''If faith does everything, and by itself suffices for justification, why then are good works commanded? Are we then to take our ease and do no works, content with faith?'' Not so, impious men, I reply; not so. That would indeed really be the case, if we were thoroughly and completely inner and spiritual persons; but that will not happen until the last day, when the dead shall be raised. As long as we live in the flesh, we are but beginning and making advances in that which shall be completed in a future life. On this account the Apostle calls that which we have in this life the first-fruits of the Spirit (Rom. viii. 23). In future we shall have the tenths, and the fullness of the Spirit. To this part belongs the fact I have stated before: that the Christian is the servant of all and subject to all. For in that part in which he is free he does no works, but in that in which he is a servant he does all works. Let us see on what principle this is so.

Although, as I have said, inwardly, and according to the spirit, a man is amply enough justified by faith, having all that he requires to have, except that this very faith and abundance ought to increase from day to day, even till the future life, still he remains in this mortal life upon earth, in which it is necessary that he should rule his own body and have intercourse with men. Here then works begin; here he must not take his ease; here he must give heed to exercise his body by fastings, watchings, labour, and other regular discipline, so that it may be subdued to the spirit, and obey and conform itself to the inner man and faith, and not rebel against them nor hinder them, as is its nature to do if it is not kept under. For the inner man, being conformed to God and created after the image of God through faith, rejoices and delights itself in Christ, in whom such blessings have been conferred on it, and hence has only this task before it: to serve God with joy and for nought in free love.

But in doing this he comes into collision with that contrary will in his own flesh, which is striving to serve the world and to seek its own gratification. This the spirit of faith cannot and will not bear, but applies itself with cheerfulness and zeal to keep it down and restrain it, as Paul says, "I delight in the law of God after the inward man; but I see another law in my members, warring against the law of my mind and bringing me into captivity to the law of sin" (Rom. vii. 22, 23), and again, "I keep under my body, and bring it unto subjection, lest that by any means, when I have preached to others, I myself should be a castaway" (I Cor. ix. 27), and "They that are Christ's have crucified the flesh, with the affections and lusts" (Gal. v. 24).

These works, however, must not be done with any notion that by them a man can be justified before God—for faith, which alone is righteousness before God, will not bear with this false notion—but solely with this purpose: that the body may be brought into subjection, and be purified from its evil lusts, so that our eyes may be turned only to purging away those lusts. For when the soul has been cleansed by faith and made to love God, it would have all things to be cleansed in like manner, and especially its own body, so that all things might unite with it in the love and praise of God. Thus it comes that, from the requirements of his own body, a man cannot take his ease, but is compelled on its account to do many good works, that he may bring it into subjection. Yet these works are not the means of his justification before God; he does them out of disinterested love to the service of God; looking to no other end than to do what is well-pleasing to Him whom he desires to obey most dutifully in all things.

On this principle every man may easily instruct himself in what measure, and with what distinctions, he ought to chasten his own body. He will fast, watch, and labour, just as much as he sees to suffice for keeping down the wantonness and concupiscence of the body. But those who pretend to be justified by works are looking, not to the mortification of their lusts, but only to the works themselves; thinking that, if they can accomplish as many works and as great ones as possible, all is well with them, and they are justified. Sometimes they even injure their brain, and extinguish nature, or at least make it useless. This is enormous folly, and ignorance of Christian life and faith, when a man seeks, without faith, to be justified and saved by works.

To make what we have said more easily understood, let us set it forth under a figure. The works of a Christian man, who is justified and saved by his faith out of the pure and unbought mercy of God, ought to be regarded in the same light as would have been those of Adam and Eve in paradise and of all their posterity if they had not sinned. Of them it is said, "The Lord God took the man and put him into the garden of Eden to dress it and to keep it" (Gen. ii. 15). Now Adam had been created by God just and righteous, so that he could not have needed to be justified and made righteous by keeping the garden and working in it; but, that he might not be unemployed, God gave him the business of keeping and cultivating paradise. These would have indeed been works of perfect freedom, being done for no object but that of pleasing God, and not in order to obtain justification, which he already had to the full, and which would have been innate in us all.

So it is with the works of a believer. Being by his faith replaced afresh in paradise and created anew, he does not need works for his justification, but that he may not be idle, but may exercise his own body and preserve it. His works are to be done freely, with the sole object of pleasing God. Only we are not yet fully created anew in perfect faith and love; these require to be increased, not, however, through works, but through themselves.

A bishop, when he consecrates a church, confirms children, or performs any other duty of his office, is not consecrated as bishop by these works; nay, unless he had been previously consecrated as bishop, not one of those works would have any validity; they would be foolish, childish, and ridiculous. Thus a Christian, being consecrated by his faith, does good works; but he is not by these works made a more sacred person, or more a Christian. This is the effect of faith alone; nay, unless he were previously a believer and a Christian, none of his works would have any value at all; they would really be impious and damnable sins.

True, then, are these two sayings: "Good works do not make a good man, but a good man does good works"; "Bad works do not make a bad man, but a bad man does bad works." Thus it is always necessary that the substance or person should be good before any good works can be done, and that good works should follow and proceed from a good person. As Christ says, "A good tree cannot bring forth evil fruit, neither can a corrupt tree bring forth good fruit" (Matt. vii. 18). Now it is clear that the fruit does not bear the tree, nor does the tree grow on the fruit; but, on the contrary, the trees bear the fruit, and the fruit grows on the trees.

As then trees must exist before their fruit, and as the fruit does not make the tree either good or bad, but on the contrary, a tree of either kind produces fruit of the same kind, so must first the person of the man be good or bad before he can do either a good or a bad work; and his works do not make him bad or good, but he himself makes his works either bad or good.

We may see the same thing in all handicrafts. A bad or good house does not make a bad or good builder, but a good or bad builder makes a good or bad house. And in general no work makes the workman such as it is itself; but the workman makes the work such as he is himself. Such is the case, too, with the works of men. Such as the man himself is, whether in faith or in unbelief, such is his work: good if it be done in faith; bad if in unbelief. But the converse is not true that, such as the work is, such the man becomes in faith or in unbelief. For as works do not make a believing man, so neither do they make a justified man; but faith, as it makes a man a believer and justified, so also it makes his works good.

Since then works justify no man, but a man must be justified before he can do any good work, it is most evident that it is faith alone which, by the mere mercy of God through Christ, and by means of His word, can worthily and sufficiently justify and save the person; and that a Christian man needs no work, no law, for his salvation; for by faith he is free from all law, and in perfect freedom does gratuitously all that he does, seeking nothing either of profit or of salvation—since by the grace of God he is already saved and rich in all things through his faith—but solely that which is well-pleasing to God.

So, too, no good work can profit an unbeliever to justification and salvation; and, on the other hand, no evil work makes him an evil and condemned person, but that unbelief, which makes the person and the tree bad, makes his works evil and condemned. Wherefore, when any man is made good or bad, this does not arise from his works, but from his faith or unbelief, as the wise man says, "The beginning of sin is to fall away from God"; that is, not to believe. Paul says, "He that cometh to God must believe" (Heb. xi. 6); and Christ says the same thing: "Either make the tree good and his fruit good; or else make the tree corrupt and his fruit corrupt" (Matt. xii. 33),—as much as to say, He who wishes to have good fruit will begin with the tree, and plant a good one; even so he who wishes to do good works must begin, not by working, but by believing, since it is this which makes the person good. For nothing makes the person good but faith, nor bad but unbelief.

It is certainly true that, in the sight of men, a man becomes good or evil by his works; but here "becoming" means that it is thus shown and recognised who is good or evil, as Christ says, "By their fruits ye shall know them" (Matt. vii. 20). But all this stops at appearances and externals; and in this matter very many deceive themselves, when they presume to write and teach that we are to be justified by good works, and meanwhile make no mention even of faith, walking in their own ways, ever deceived and deceiving, going from bad to worse, blind leaders of the blind, wearying themselves with many works, and yet never attaining to true righteousness, of whom Paul says, "Having a form of godliness, but denying the power thereof, ever learning and never able to come to the knowledge of the truth" (2 Tim. iii. 5, 7).

He then who does not wish to go astray, with these blind ones, must look further than to the works of the law or the doctrine of works; nay, must turn away his sight from works, and look to the person, and to the manner in which it may be justified. Now it is justified and saved, not by works or laws, but by the word of God—that is, by the promise of His grace—so that the glory may be to the Divine majesty, which has saved us who believe, not by works of righteousness which we have done, but according to His mercy, by the word of His grace.

From all this it is easy to perceive on what principle good works are to be cast aside or embraced, and by what rule all teachings put forth concerning works are to be understood. For if works are brought forward as grounds of justification, and are done under the false persuasion that we can pretend to be justified by them, they lay on us the yoke of necessity, and extinguish liberty along with faith, and by this very addition to their use they become no longer good, but really worthy of condemnation. For such works are not free, but blaspheme the grace of God, to which alone it belongs to justify and save through faith. Works cannot accomplish this, and yet, with impious presumption, through our folly, they take it on themselves to do so; and thus break in with violence upon the office and glory of grace.

We do not then reject good works; nay, we embrace them and teach them in the highest degree. It is not on their own account that we condemn them, but on account of this impious addition to them and the perverse notion of seeking justification by them. These things cause them to be only good in outward show, but in reality not good, since by them men are deceived and deceive others, like ravening wolves in sheep's clothing.

Now this leviathan, this perverted notion about works, is invincible when sincere faith is wanting. For those sanctified doers of works cannot but hold it till faith, which destroys it, comes and reigns in the heart. Nature cannot expel it by her own power; nay, cannot even see it for what it is, but considers it as a most holy will. And when custom steps in besides, and strengthens this pravity of nature, as has happened by means of impious teachers, then the evil is incurable, and leads astray multitudes to irreparable ruin. Therefore, though it is good to preach and write about penitence, confession, and satisfaction, yet if we stop there, and do not go on to teach faith, such teaching is without doubt deceitful and devilish. For Christ, speaking by His servant John, not only said, "Repent ye," but added, "For the kingdom of heaven is at hand" (Matt. iii. 2).

For not one word of God only, but both, should be preached; new and old things should be brought out of the treasury, as well the voice of the law as the word of grace. The voice of the law should be brought forward, that men may be terrified and brought to a knowledge of their sins, and thence be converted to penitence and to a better manner of life. But we must not stop here; that would be to wound only and not to bind up, to strike and not to heal, to kill and not to make alive, to bring down to hell and not to bring back, to humble and not to exalt. Therefore, the word of grace and of the promised remission of sin must also be preached, in order to teach and set up faith, since without that word contrition, penitence, and all other duties, are performed and taught in vain.

There still remain, it is true, preachers of repentance and grace, but they do not explain the law and the promises of God to such an end, and in such a spirit, that men may learn whence repentance and grace are to come. For repentance comes from the law of God, but faith or grace from the promises of God, as it is said, "Faith cometh by hearing, and hearing by the word of God" (Rom. x. 17), whence it comes that a man, when humbled and brought to the knowledge of himself by the threatenings and terrors of the law, is consoled and raised up by faith in the Divine promise. Thus "weeping may endure for a night, but joy cometh in the morning" (Psalm xxx. 5). Thus much we say concerning works in general, and also concerning those which the Christian practises with regard to his own body.

Lastly, we will speak also of those works which he performs towards his neighbour. For man does not live for himself alone in this mortal body, in order to work on its account, but also for all men on earth; nay, he lives only for others, and not for himself. For it is to this end that he brings his own body into subjection, that he may be able to serve others more sincerely and more freely, as Paul says, "none of us liveth to himself, and no man dieth to himself. For whether we live, we live unto the Lord; and whether we die, we die unto the Lord" (Rom. xiv. 7, 8). Thus it is impossible that he should take his ease in this life, and not work for the good of his neighbours, since he must needs speak, act, and converse among men, just as Christ was made in the likeness of men and found in fashion as a man, and had His conversation among men.

Yet a Christian has need of none of these things for justification and salvation, but in all his works he ought to entertain this view and look only to this object—that he may serve and be useful to others in all that he does; having nothing before his eyes but the necessities and the advantage of his neighbour. Thus the Apostle commands us to work with our own hands, that we may have to give to those that need. He might have said, that we may support ourselves; but he tells us to give to those that need. It is the part of a Christian to take care of his own body for the very purpose that, by its soundness and well-being, he may be enabled to labour, and to acquire and preserve property, for the aid of those who are in want, that thus the stronger member may serve the weaker member, and we may be children of God, thoughtful and busy one for another, bearing one another's burdens, and so fulfilling the law of Christ.

Here is the truly Christian life, here is faith really working by love, when a man applies himself with joy and love to the works of that freest servitude in which he serves others voluntarily and for nought, himself abundantly satisfied in the fulness and riches of his own faith.

Thus, when Paul had taught the Philippians how they had been made rich by that faith in Christ in which they had obtained all things, he teaches them further in these words: "If there be therefore any consolation in Christ, if any comfort of love, if any fellowship of the Spirit, if any bowels and mercies, fulfil ye my joy, that ye be like-minded, having the same love, being of one accord, of one mind. Let nothing be done through strife or vain-glory; but in lowliness of mind let each esteem other better than themselves. Look not every man on his own things, but every man also on the things of others" (Phil. ii. 1-4).

In this we see clearly that the Apostle lays down this rule for a Christian life: that all our works should be directed to the advantage of others, since every Christian has such abundance through his faith that all his other works and his whole life remain over and above wherewith to serve and benefit his neighbour of spontaneous goodwill.

To this end he brings forward Christ as an example, saying, "Let this mind be in you, which was also in Christ Jesus, who, being in the form of God, thought it not robbery to be equal with God, but made Himself of no reputation, and took upon Him the form of a servant, and was made in the likeness of men; and being found in fashion as a man, He humbled Himself, and became obedient unto death" (Phil. ii. 5-8). This most wholesome saying of the Apostle has been darkened to us by men who, totally misunderstanding the expressions "form of God," "form of a servant," "fashion," "likeness of men," have transferred them to the natures of Godhead and manhood. Paul's meaning is this: Christ, when He was full of the form of God and abounded in all good things, so that He had no need of works or sufferings to be just and saved—for all these things He had from the very beginning—yet was not puffed up with these things, and did not raise Himself above us and arrogate to Himself power over us, though He might lawfully have done so, but, on the contrary, so acted in labouring, working, suffering, and dying, as to be like the rest of men, and no otherwise than a man in fashion and in conduct, as if He were in want of all things and had nothing of the form of God; and yet all this He did for our sakes, that He might serve us, and that all the works He should do under that form of a servant might become ours.

Thus a Christian, like Christ his Head, being full and in abundance through his faith, ought to be content with this form of God, obtained by faith; except that, as I have said, he ought to increase this faith till it be perfected. For this faith is his life, justification, and salvation, preserving his person itself and making it pleasing to God, and bestowing on him all that Christ has, as I have said above, and as Paul affirms: "The life which I now live in the flesh I live by the faith of the Son of God" (Gal. ii. 20). Though he is thus free from all works, yet he ought to empty himself of this liberty, take on him the form of a servant, be made in the likeness of men, be found in fashion as a man, serve, help, and in every way act towards his neighbour as he sees that God through Christ has acted and is acting towards him. All this he should do freely, and with regard to nothing but the good pleasure of God, and he should reason thus:—

Lo! my God, without merit on my part, of His pure and free mercy, has given to me, an unworthy, condemned, and contemptible creature all the riches of justification and salvation in Christ, so that I no longer am in want of anything, except of faith to believe that this is so. For such a Father, then, who has overwhelmed me with these inestimable riches of His, why should I not freely, cheerfully, and with my whole heart, and from voluntary zeal, do all that I know will be pleasing to Him and acceptable in His sight? I will therefore give myself as a sort of Christ, to my neighbour, as Christ has given Himself to me; and will do nothing in this life except what I see will be needful, advantageous, and wholesome for my neighbour, since by faith I abound in all good things in Christ.

Thus from faith flow love and joy in the Lord, and from love a cheerful, willing, free spirit, disposed to serve our neighbour voluntarily, without taking any account of gratitude or ingratitude, praise or blame, gain or loss. Its object is not to lay men under obligations, nor does it distinguish between friends and enemies, or look to gratitude or ingratitude, but most freely and willingly spends itself and its goods, whether it loses them through ingratitude, or gains goodwill. For thus did its Father, distributing all things to all men abundantly and freely, making His sun to rise upon the just and the unjust. Thus, too, the child does and endures nothing except from the free joy with which it delights through Christ in God, the Giver of such great gifts.

You see, then, that, if we recognize those great and precious gifts, as Peter says, which have been given to us, love is quickly diffused in our hearts through the Spirit, and by love we are made free, joyful, all-powerful, active workers, victors over all our tribulations, servants to our neighbour, and nevertheless lords of all things. But; for those who do not recognize the good things given to them through Christ, Christ has been born in vain; such persons walk by works, and will never attain the taste and feeling of these great things. Therefore just as our neighbour is in want, and has need of our abundance, so we too in the sight of God were in want and had need of His mercy. And as our heavenly Father has freely helped us in Christ, so ought we freely to help our neighbour by our body and works, and each should become to other a sort of Christ, so that we may be mutually Christs, and that the same Christ may be in all of us; that is, that we may be truly Christians.

Who then can comprehend the riches and glory of the Christian life? It can do all things, has all things, and is in want of nothing; is lord over sin, death, and hell, and at the same time is the obedient and useful servant of all. But alas! it is at this day unknown throughout the world; it is neither preached nor sought after, so that we are quite ignorant about our own name, why we are and are called Christians. We are certainly called so from Christ, who is not absent, but dwells among us—provided, that is, that we believe in Him and are reciprocally and mutually one the Christ of the other, doing to our neighbour as Christ does to us. But now, in the doctrine of men, we are taught only to seek after merits, rewards, and things which are already ours, and we have made of Christ a taskmaster far more severe than Moses.

The Blessed Virgin beyond all others, affords us an example of the same faith, in that she was purified according to the law of Moses, and like all other women, though she was bound by no such law and had no need of purification. Still she submitted to the law voluntarily and of free love, making herself like the rest of women, that she might not offend or throw contempt on them. She was not justified by doing this; but, being already justified, she did it freely and gratuitously. Thus ought our works too to be done, and not in order to be justified by them; for, being first justified by faith, we ought to do all our works freely and cheerfully for the sake of others.

St. Paul circumcised his disciple Timothy, not because he needed circumcision for his justification, but that he might not offend or contemn those Jews, weak in the faith, who had not yet been able to comprehend the liberty of faith. On the other hand, when they contemned liberty and urged that circumcision was necessary for justification, he resisted them, and would not allow Titus to be circumcised. For, as he would not offend or contemn any one's weakness in faith, but yielded for the time to their will, so, again, he would not have the liberty of faith offended or contemned by hardened self-justifiers, but walked in a middle path, sparing the weak for the time, and always resisting the hardened, that he might convert all to the liberty of faith. On the same principle we ought to act, receiving those that are weak in the faith, but boldly resisting these hardened teachers of works, of whom we shall hereafter speak at more length.

Christ also, when His disciples were asked for the tribute money, asked of Peter whether the children of a king were not free from taxes. Peter agreed to this; yet Jesus commanded him to go to the sea, saying, "Lest we should offend them, go thou to the sea, and cast a hook, and take up the fish that first cometh up; and when thou hast opened his mouth thou shalt find a piece of money; that take, and give unto them for Me and thee" (Matt. xvii. 27).

This example is very much to our purpose; for here Christ calls Himself and His disciples free men and children of a King, in want of nothing; and yet He voluntarily submits and pays the tax. Just as far, then, as this work was necessary or useful to Christ for justification or salvation, so far do all His other works or those of His disciples avail for justification. They are really free and subsequent to justification, and only done to serve others and set them an example.

Such are the works which Paul inculcated, that Christians should be subject to principalities and powers and ready to every good work (Titus iii. 1), not that they may be justified by these things—for they are already justified by faith—but that in liberty of spirit they may thus be the servants of others and subject to powers, obeying their will out of gratuitous love.

Such, too, ought to have been the works of all colleges, monasteries, and priests; every one doing the works of his own profession and state of life, not in order to be justified by them, but in order to bring his own body into subjection, as an example to others, who themselves also need to keep under their bodies, and also in order to accommodate himself to the will of others, out of free love. But we must always guard most carefully against any vain confidence or presumption of being justified, gaining merit, or being saved by these works, this being the part of faith alone, as I have so often said.

Any man possessing this knowledge may easily keep clear of danger among those innumerable commands and precepts of the Pope, of bishops, of monasteries, of churches, of princes, and of magistrates, which some foolish pastors urge on us as being necessary for justification and salvation, calling them precepts of the Church, when they are not so at all. For the Christian freeman will speak thus: I will fast, I will pray, I will do this or that which is commanded me by men, not as having any need of these things for justification or salvation, but that I may thus comply with the will of the Pope, of the bishop, of such a community or such a magistrate, or of my neighbour as an example to him; for this cause I will do and suffer all things, just as Christ did and suffered much more for me, though He needed not at all to do so on His own account, and made Himself for my sake under the law, when He was not under the law. And although tyrants may do me violence or wrong in requiring obedience to these things, yet it will not hurt me to do them, so long as they are not done against God.

From all this every man will be able to attain a sure judgment and faithful discrimination between all works and laws, and to know who are blind and foolish pastors, and who are true and good ones. For whatsoever work is not directed to the sole end either of keeping under the body, or of doing service to our neighbour—provided he require nothing contrary to the will of God—is no good or Christian work. Hence I greatly fear that at this day few or no colleges, monasteries, altars, or ecclesiastical functions are Christian ones; and the same may be said of fasts and special prayers to certain saints. I fear that in all these, nothing is being sought but what is already ours; while we fancy that by these things our sins are purged away and salvation is attained, and thus utterly do away with Christian liberty. This comes from ignorance of Christian faith and liberty.

This ignorance and this crushing of liberty are diligently promoted by the teaching of very many blind pastors, who stir up and urge the people to a zeal for these things, praising them and puffing them up with their indulgences, but never teaching faith. Now I would advise you, if you have any wish to pray, to fast, or to make foundations in churches, as they call it, to take care not to do so with the object of gaining any advantage, either temporal or eternal. You will thus wrong your faith, which alone bestows all things on you, and the increase of which, either by working or by suffering, is alone to be cared for. What you give, give freely and without price, that others may prosper and have increase from you and your goodness. Thus you will be a truly good man and a Christian. For what to you are your goods and your works, which are done over and above for the subjection of the body, since you have abundance for yourself through your faith, in which God has given you all things?

We give this rule: the good things which we have from God ought to flow from one to another and become common to all, so that every one of us may, as it were, put on his neighbour, and so behave towards him as if he were himself in his place. They flowed and do flow from Christ to us; He put us on, and acted for us as if He Himself were what we are. From us they flow to those who have need of them; so that my faith and righteousness ought to be laid down before God as a covering and intercession for the sins of my neighbour, which I am to take on myself, and so labour and endure servitude in them, as if they were my own; for thus has Christ done for us. This is true love and the genuine truth of Christian life. But only there is it true and genuine where there is true and genuine faith. Hence the Apostle attributes to charity this quality: that she seeketh not her own.

We conclude therefore that a Christian man does not live in himself, but in Christ and in his neighbour, or else is no Christian: in Christ by faith; in his neighbour by love. By faith he is carried upwards above himself to God, and by love he sinks back below himself to his neighbour, still always abiding in God and His love, as Christ says, "Verily I say unto you, Hereafter ye shall see heaven open, and the angels of God ascending and descending upon the Son of man" (John i. 51).

Thus much concerning liberty, which, as you see, is a true and spiritual liberty, making our hearts free from all sins, laws, and commandments, as Paul says, "The law is not made for a righteous man" (I Tim. i. 9), and one which surpasses all other external liberties, as far as heaven is above earth. May Christ make us to understand and preserve this liberty. Amen.

Finally, for the sake of those to whom nothing can be stated so well but that they misunderstand and distort it, we must add a word, in case they can understand even that. There are very many persons who, when they hear of this liberty of faith, straightway turn it into an occasion of licence. They think that everything is now lawful for them, and do not choose to show themselves free men and Christians in any other way than by their contempt and reprehension of ceremonies, of traditions, of human laws; as if they were Christians merely because they refuse to fast on stated days, or eat flesh when others fast, or omit the customary prayers; scoffing at the precepts of men, but utterly passing over all the rest that belongs to the Christian religion. On the other hand, they are most pertinaciously resisted by those who strive after salvation solely by their observance of and reverence for ceremonies, as if they would be saved merely because they fast on stated days, or abstain from flesh, or make formal prayers; talking loudly of the precepts of the Church and of the Fathers, and not caring a straw about those things which belong to our genuine faith. Both these parties are plainly culpable, in that, while they neglect matters which are of weight and necessary for salvation, they contend noisily about such as are without weight and not necessary.

How much more rightly does the Apostle Paul teach us to walk in the middle path, condemning either extreme and saying, "Let not him that eateth despise him that eateth not; and let not him which eateth not judge him that eateth" (Rom. xiv. 3)! You see here how the Apostle blames those who, not from religious feeling, but in mere contempt, neglect and rail at ceremonial observances, and teaches them not to despise, since this "knowledge puffeth up." Again, he teaches the pertinacious upholders of these things not to judge their opponents. For neither party observes towards the other that charity which edifieth. In this matter we must listen to Scripture, which teaches us to turn aside neither to the right hand nor to the left, but to follow those right precepts of the Lord which rejoice the heart. For just as a man is not righteous merely because he serves and is devoted to works and ceremonial rites, so neither will he be accounted righteous merely because he neglects and despises them.

It is not from works that we are set free by the faith of Christ, but from the belief in works, that is from foolishly presuming to seek justification through works. Faith redeems our consciences, makes them upright, and preserves them, since by it we recognize the truth that justification does not depend on our works, although good works neither can nor ought to be absent, just as we cannot exist without food and drink and all the functions of this mortal body. Still it is not on them that our justification is based, but on faith; and yet they ought not on that account to be despised or neglected. Thus in this world we are compelled by the needs of this bodily life; but we are not hereby justified. "My kingdom is not hence, nor of this world," says Christ; but He does not say, "My kingdom is not here, nor in this world." Paul, too, says, "Though we walk in the flesh, we do not war after the flesh" (2 Cor. x. 3), and "The life which I now live in the flesh I live by the faith of the Son of God" (Gal. ii. 20). Thus our doings, life, and being, in works and ceremonies, are done from the necessities of this life, and with the motive of governing our bodies; but yet we are not justified by these things, but by the faith of the Son of God.

The Christian must therefore walk in the middle path, and set these two classes of men before his eyes. He may meet with hardened and obstinate ceremonialists, who, like deaf adders, refuse to listen to the truth of liberty, and cry up, enjoin, and urge on us their ceremonies, as if they could justify us without faith. Such were the Jews of old, who would not understand, that they might act well. These men we must resist, do just the contrary to what they do, and be bold to give them offence, lest by this impious notion of theirs they should deceive many along with themselves. Before the eyes of these men it is expedient to eat flesh, to break fasts, and to do in behalf of the liberty of faith things which they hold to be the greatest sins. We must say of them, "Let them alone; they be blind leaders of the blind" (Matt. xv. 14). In this way Paul also would not have Titus circumcised, though these men urged it; and Christ defended the Apostles, who had plucked ears of corn on the Sabbath day; and many like instances.

Or else we may meet with simple-minded and ignorant persons, weak in the faith, as the Apostle calls them, who are as yet unable to apprehend that liberty of faith, even if willing to do so. These we must spare, lest they should be offended. We must bear with their infirmity, till they shall be more fully instructed. For since these men do not act thus from hardened malice, but only from weakness of faith, therefore, in order to avoid giving them offence, we must keep fasts and do other things which they consider necessary. This is required of us by charity, which injures no one, but serves all men. It is not the fault of these persons that they are weak, but that of their pastors, who by the snares and weapons of their own traditions have brought them into bondage and wounded their souls when they ought to have been set free and healed by the teaching of faith and liberty. Thus the Apostle says, "If meat make my brother to offend, I will eat no flesh while the world standeth" (I Cor. viii. 13); and again, "I know, and am persuaded by the Lord Jesus, that there is nothing unclean of itself; but to him that esteemeth anything to be unclean, to him it is unclean. It is evil for that man who eateth with offence" (Rom. xiv. 14, 20).

Thus, though we ought boldly to resist those teachers of tradition, and though the laws of the pontiffs, by which they make aggressions on the people of God, deserve sharp reproof, yet we must spare the timid crowd, who are held captive by the laws of those impious tyrants, till they are set free. Fight vigorously against the wolves, but on behalf of the sheep, not against the sheep. And this you may do by inveighing against the laws and lawgivers, and yet at the same time observing these laws with the weak, lest they be offended, until they shall themselves recognize the tyranny, and understand their own liberty. If you wish to use your liberty, do it secretly, as Paul says, "Hast thou faith? have it to thyself before God" (Rom. xiv. 22). But take care not to use it in the presence of the weak. On the other hand, in the presence of tyrants and obstinate opposers, use your liberty in their despite, and with the utmost pertinacity, that they too may understand that they are tyrants, and their laws useless for justification, nay that they had no right to establish such laws.

Since then we cannot live in this world without ceremonies and works, since the hot and inexperienced period of youth has need of being restrained and protected by such bonds, and since every one is bound to keep under his own body by attention to these things, therefore the minister of Christ must be prudent and faithful in so ruling and teaching the people of Christ, in all these matters, that no root of bitterness may spring up among them, and so many be defiled, as Paul warned the Hebrews; that is, that they may not lose the faith, and begin to be defiled by a belief in works as the means of justification. This is a thing which easily happens, and defiles very many, unless faith be constantly inculcated along with works. It is impossible to avoid this evil, when faith is passed over in silence, and only the ordinances of men are taught, as has been done hitherto by the pestilent, impious, and soul-destroying traditions of our pontiffs and opinions of our theologians. An infinite number of souls have been drawn down to hell by these snares, so that you may recognize the work of antichrist.

In brief, as poverty is imperilled amid riches, honesty amid business, humility amid honours, abstinence amid feasting, purity amid pleasures, so is justification by faith imperilled among ceremonies. Solomon says, "Can a man take fire in his bosom, and his clothes not be burned?" (Prov. vi. 27). And yet as we must live among riches, business, honours, pleasures, feastings, so must we among ceremonies, that is among perils. Just as infant boys have the greatest need of being cherished in the bosoms and by the care of girls, that they may not die, and yet, when they are grown, there is peril to their salvation in living among girls, so inexperienced and fervid young men require to be kept in and restrained by the barriers of ceremonies, even were they of iron, lest their weak minds should rush headlong into vice. And yet it would be death to them to persevere in believing that they can be justified by these things. They must rather be taught that they have been thus imprisoned, not with the purpose of their being justified or gaining merit in this way, but in order that they might avoid wrong-doing, and be more easily instructed in that righteousness which is by faith, a thing which the headlong character of youth would not bear unless it were put under restraint.

Hence in the Christian life ceremonies are to be no otherwise looked upon than as builders and workmen look upon those preparations for building or working which are not made with any view of being permanent or anything in themselves, but only because without them there could be no building and no work. When the structure is completed, they are laid aside. Here you see that we do not contemn these preparations, but set the highest value on them; a belief in them we do contemn, because no one thinks that they constitute a real and permanent structure. If any one were so manifestly out of his senses as to have no other object in life but that of setting up these preparations with all possible expense, diligence, and perseverance, while he never thought of the structure itself, but pleased himself and made his boast of these useless preparations and props, should we not all pity his madness and think that, at the cost thus thrown away, some great building might have been raised?

Thus, too, we do not contemn works and ceremonies—nay, we set the highest value on them; but we contemn the belief in works, which no one should consider to constitute true righteousness, as do those hypocrites who employ and throw away their whole life in the pursuit of works, and yet never attain to that for the sake of which the works are done. As the Apostle says, they are "ever learning and never able to come to the knowledge of the truth" (2 Tim. iii. 7). They appear to wish to build, they make preparations, and yet they never do build; and thus they continue in a show of godliness, but never attain to its power.

Meanwhile they please themselves with this zealous pursuit, and even dare to judge all others, whom they do not see adorned with such a glittering display of works; while, if they had been imbued with faith, they might have done great things for their own and others' salvation, at the same cost which they now waste in abuse of the gifts of God. But since human nature and natural reason, as they call it, are naturally superstitious, and quick to believe that justification can be attained by any laws or works proposed to them, and since nature is also exercised and confirmed in the same view by the practice of all earthly law-givers, she can never of her own power free herself from this bondage to works, and come to a recognition of the liberty of faith.

We have therefore need to pray that God will lead us and make us taught of God, that is, ready to learn from God; and will Himself, as He has promised, write His law in our hearts; otherwise there is no hope for us. For unless He Himself teach us inwardly this wisdom hidden in a mystery, nature cannot but condemn it and judge it to be heretical. She takes offence at it, and it seems folly to her, just as we see that it happened of old in the case of the prophets and Apostles, and just as blind and impious pontiffs, with their flatterers, do now in my case and that of those who are like me, upon whom, together with ourselves, may God at length have mercy, and lift up the light of His countenance upon them, that we may know His way upon earth and His saving health among all nations, who is blessed for evermore. Amen. In the year of the Lord MDXX.

ENCHIRIDION.

THE SMALL CATECHISM

OF

Dr. MARTIN LUTHER.

FOR PASTORS AND PREACHERS.

PREFACE.

MARTIN LUTHER TO ALL FAITHFUL, PIOUS PASTORS AND PREACHERS: GRACE, MERCY, AND PEACE IN CHRIST JESUS, OUR LORD!

The deplorable destitution which I recently observed, during a visitation of the churches, has impelled and constrained me to prepare this Catechism or Christian Doctrine in such a small and simple form. Alas, what manifold misery I beheld! The common people, especially in the villages, know nothing at all of Christian doctrine; and many pastors are quite unfit and incompetent to teach. Yet all are called Christians, have been baptized, and enjoy the use of the Sacraments, although they know neither the Lord's Prayer, nor the Creed, nor the Ten Commandments, and live like the poor brutes and irrational swine. Still they have, now that the Gospel has come, learned to abuse all liberty in a masterly manner.

O ye bishops! how will ye ever render account to Christ for having so shamefully neglected the people, and having never for a moment exercised your office! May the judgment not overtake you! You command communion in one kind, and urge your human ordinances; but never ask, in the meantime, whether the people know the Lord's Prayer, the Creed, the Ten Commandments, or any part of God's Word. Woe, woe unto you everlastingly!

Therefore I entreat you all, for God's sake, my dear brethren who are pastors and preachers, to devote yourselves heartily to your office, and have pity upon the people who are committed to your charge. Help us to inculcate the Catechism upon them, especially upon the young. Let those who are not able to do better take these tables and forms and set them word for word before the people, in the manner following:—

First, the minister should above all things avoid the use of different texts and forms of the Ten Commandments, the Lord's Prayer, the Creed, the Sacraments, etc. Let him adopt one form and adhere to it, using it one year as the other; for young and ignorant people must be taught one certain text and form, and will easily become confused if we teach thus to-day and otherwise next year, as if we thought of making improvements. In this way all effort and labor will be lost. This our honored fathers well understood, who all used the Lord's Prayer, the Creed, the Ten Commandments in one and the same manner. Therefore we also should so teach these forms to the young and inexperienced as not to change a syllable, nor set them forth and recite them one year differently from the other.

Hence choose whatever form you think best, and adhere to it forever. When you preach among the learned and judicious, you may show your art, and set these things forth with as many flourishes, and turn them as skillfully as you wish; but among the young adhere to one and the same fixed form and manner, and teach them, first of all, the text of the Ten Commandments, the Creed, the Lord's Prayer, etc., so that they can say it after you word for word, and commit it to memory.

But those who are unwilling to learn it should be told that they deny Christ and are no Christians; neither should they be admitted to the Sacrament, accepted as sponsors at baptism, nor be accorded the exercise of Christian liberty; but they are simply to be remanded to the pope and his officials, yea, to the devil himself. Parents and employers should also refuse them meat and drink, and give them to understand that the prince will drive such rude fellows from the country. For although we cannot and should not force any one to believe, yet we should lead and urge the masses to perceive what those consider right and wrong among whom they live and find their sustenance. Whoever would live in a city and enjoy its privileges, should know and observe its laws, whether he believe or be at heart a rogue or knave.

Secondly, when they have well learned the text, teach them the sense also, that they may know what it means. Again take the form of these tables or some other short fixed form of your choice, and adhere to it without the change of a single syllable, as was said of the text; and take your time to it; for it is not necessary to take up all the parts at once, but take one after the other. When they well understand the first Commandment, proceed to the second, and thus continue; otherwise they will be overburdened, and be able to retain nothing well.

Thirdly, after you have taught them this short Catechism, take up the Large Catechism, and impart to them a richer and fuller knowledge; dwell on each commandment, petition, and part, with its various works, uses, benefits, dangers, and harm, as you may find these abundantly pointed out in many books treating of these subjects; and especially give most attention to the Commandment or part which is most neglected among your people. For example, the seventh Commandment, which forbids stealing, you must particularly inforce among mechanics and merchants, and also among farmers and servants; for among such people all kinds of unfaithfulness and thieving are frequent. Again, you must urge the fourth Commandment among children and the common people, that they may be quiet, faithful, obedient, peaceable, always adducing frequent examples from the Scriptures to show how God punished or blessed such persons.

Especially should you here urge civil rulers and parents to govern well and educate children for service in schools, showing them their duty in this regard, and the greatness of their sin if they neglect it; for by such neglect they overthrow and destroy both the kingdom of God and that of this world, and show themselves to be the worst foes both of God and man. Dwell on the great harm they do, if they will not help to educate children for the ministry, clerkships, and other offices, etc., and on the terrible punishment God will visit upon them for it. It is necessary to preach of these things; for parents and rulers sin unspeakably in them, and the devil has a horrible object in view.

Lastly, since the people are freed from the tyranny of the pope, they no longer desire to go to the Sacrament, but despise it. It is necessary to be urgent on this point, remembering, however, that we are to force no one to believe, or to receive the Sacrament, nor to fix any law, time, or place for it; but so to preach, that they will be urged of their own accord, without our law, and will, as it were, compel us pastors to administer the Sacrament. This is done by telling them that if a person does not seek nor desire the Lord's Supper at least some four times a year, it is to be feared that he despises the Sacrament and is not a Christian, just as he is not a Christian who refuses to believe or to hear the Gospel. For Christ did not say, Omit this, or, Despise this; but, This do ye, as oft as ye drink it, etc. Truly, He wants it done, and by no means neglected or despised: "This do ye," is His command.

Whoever does not highly prize the Sacrament, thus shows that he has no sin, no flesh, no devil, no world, no death, no danger, no hell; that is, he does not believe that they exist, although he is in them over head and ears, and is doubly the devil's. On the other hand, he needs no grace, life, Paradise, heaven, Christ, God, nor anything good: for if he believed that he has so much that is evil, and needs so much that is good, he would not thus neglect the Sacrament, by which such evil is remedied and so much good is bestowed. Neither would it be necessary to force him to the Sacrament by any law, but he would hasten to it of his own accord, and constrain himself and compel you to administer it to him.

Therefore you need not make any law in this matter, as the pope does; only set forth clearly the benefit and harm, the necessity and use, the danger and blessing, connected with this Sacrament, and the people will come of themselves, without your compulsion. But if they do not come, let them alone, telling them that they are of the devil, as they do not regard nor feel their great need, and God's gracious help. Should you, however, fail to urge this matter, or make a law or a bane of it, it is your fault if they despise the Sacrament. How could they be otherwise than slothful, if you sleep and keep silence? Therefore look to it, ye pastors and preachers; our office is a different thing now from what it was under the pope; it has now become earnest and salutary. Hence it involves much more trouble and labour, danger and trial, and secures but little reward and gratitude in the world. But Christ Himself will be our reward, if we labor faithfully. To this end may the Father of all grace help us, to whom be praise and thanks in eternity, through Christ our Lord! Amen.

The Ten Commandments,

AS THE HEAD OF THE FAMILY SHOULD TEACH THEM IN ALL SIMPLICITY TO HIS HOUSEHOLD.

THE FIRST COMMANDMENT,

Thou shalt have no other gods before me.

What does this mean? Answer:

We should fear, love, and trust in God above all things.

THE SECOND COMMANDMENT.

Thou shalt not take the name of the Lord thy God in vain.

What does this mean? Answer:

We should fear and love God, that we may not curse, swear, use witchcraft, lie, or deceive by His name; but call upon it in every trouble, pray, praise, and give thanks.

THE THIRD COMMANDMENT.

Thou shalt sanctify the holy-day.

What does this mean? Answer:

We should fear and love God, that we may not despise preaching and His Word; but hold it sacred, and gladly hear and learn it.

THE FOURTH COMMANDMENT.

Thou shalt honor thy father and thy mother, that it may be well with thee, and thou mayest live long on the earth.

What does this mean? Answer:

We should fear and love God, that we may not despise our parents and masters, nor provoke them to anger; but give them honor, serve and obey them, and hold them in love and esteem.

THE FIFTH COMMANDMENT.

Thou shalt not kill.

What does this mean? Answer:

We should fear and love God, that we may not hurt nor harm our neighbor in his body; but help and befriend him in every bodily need.

THE SIXTH COMMANDMENT.

Thou shalt not commit adultery.

What does this mean? Answer:

We should fear and love God, that we may lead a chaste and decent life in word and deed, and each love and honor his spouse.

THE SEVENTH COMMANDMENT.

Thou shalt not steal.

What does this mean? Answer:

We should fear and love God, that we may not take our neighbor's money or goods, nor get them by false ware or dealing; but help him to improve and protect his property and business.

THE EIGHTH COMMANDMENT.

Thou shalt not bear false witness against thy neighbor.

What does this mean? Answer:

We should fear and love God, that we may not deceitfully belie, betray, slander, nor defame our neighbor; but defend him, speak well of him, and put the best construction on everything.

THE NINTH COMMANDMENT.

Thou shalt not covet thy neighbor's house.

What does this mean? Answer:

We should fear and love God, that we may not craftily seek to get our neighbor's inheritance or house, nor obtain it by a show of right; but help and be of service to him in keeping it.

THE TENTH COMMANDMENT.

Thou shalt not covet thy neighbor's wife, nor his man-servant, nor his maid-servant, nor his cattle, nor anything that is thy neighbor's.

What does this mean? Answer:

We should fear and love God, that we may not estrange, force, or entice away from our neighbor his wife, servants, or cattle; but urge them to stay and do their duty.

What does God say of all these commandments? Answer:

He says thus: I the Lord thy God am a jealous God, visiting the iniquity of the fathers upon the children unto the third and fourth generation of them that hate me, and showing mercy unto thousands of them that love me and keep my commandments.

What does this mean? Answer:

God threatens to punish all that transgress these commandments. Therefore we should fear His wrath, and not act contrary to them. But He promises grace and every blessing to all that keep these commandments. Therefore we should also love and trust in Him, and willingly do according to His commandments.

The Creed,

AS THE HEAD OF THE FAMILY SHOULD TEACH IT IN ALL SIMPLICITY TO HIS HOUSEHOLD.

THE FIRST ARTICLE.

OF CREATION.

I believe in God the Father Almighty,
Maker of heaven and earth.

What does this mean? Answer:

I believe that God has made me and all creatures; that He has given me my body and soul, eyes, ears, and all my members, my reason and all my senses, and still preserves them; also clothing and shoes, meat and drink, house and home, wife and children, fields, cattle, and all my goods; that He richly and daily provides me with all that I need to support this body and life; that He defends me against all danger, and guards and protects me from all evil; and all this purely out of fatherly, divine goodness and mercy, without any merit or worthiness in me; for all which it is my duty to thank and praise, to serve and obey Him. This is most certainly true.

THE SECOND ARTICLE.

OF REDEMPTION.

And in Jesus Christ, His only Son, our Lord, who was conceived by the Holy Ghost, born of the Virgin Mary, suffered under

Pontius Pilate, was crucified, dead, and buried; He descended into hell; the third day He rose again from the dead; He ascended into heaven, and sitteth at the right hand of God the Father Almighty, from thence He shall come to judge the quick and the dead.

What does this mean? Answer:

I believe that Jesus Christ, true God, begotten of the Father from eternity, and also true man, born of the Virgin Mary, is my Lord, who has redeemed me, a lost and condemned creature, purchased and won me from all sins, from death, and from the power of the devil, not with gold or silver, but with His holy precious blood and with His innocent suffering and death, that I may be His own, and live under Him in His kingdom, and serve Him in everlasting righteousness, innocence, and blessedness, even as He is risen from the dead, lives and reigns to all eternity. This is most certainly true.

THE THIRD ARTICLE.
OF SANCTIFICATION.

I believe in the Holy Ghost; the holy Christian Church, the communion of saints; the forgiveness of sins; the resurrection of the body; and the life everlasting. Amen.

What does this mean? Answer:

I believe that I cannot by my own reason or strength believe in Jesus Christ, my Lord, or come to Him; but the Holy Ghost has called me by the Gospel, enlightened me with His gifts, sanctified and kept me in the true faith; even as He calls, gathers, enlightens, and sanctifies the whole Christian Church on earth, and keeps it with Jesus Christ in the one true faith: in which Christian Church He daily and richly forgives all sins to me and all believers, and will at the last day raise up me and all the dead, and give unto me and all believers in Christ eternal life. This is most certainly true.

The Lord's Prayer,

AS THE HEAD OF THE FAMILY SHOULD TEACH IT IN ALL SIMPLICITY TO HIS HOUSEHOLD.

Our Father who art in heaven.

What does this mean? Answer:

God would by these words tenderly invite us to believe that He is our true Father, and that we are His true children, so that we may with all boldness and confidence ask Him, as dear children ask their dear father.

THE FIRST PETITION.

Hallowed be Thy name.

What does this mean? Answer:

God's name is indeed holy in itself; but we pray in this petition that it may be holy among us also.

How is this done? Answer:

When the Word of God is taught in its truth and purity, and we as the children of God also lead a holy life according to it. This grant us, dear Father in heaven. But he that teaches and lives otherwise than God's Word teaches, profanes the name of God among us. From this preserve us, Heavenly Father.

THE SECOND PETITION.

Thy kingdom come.

What does this mean? Answer:

The kingdom of God comes indeed without our prayer, of itself; but we pray in this petition that it may come unto us also.

How is this done? Answer:

When our Heavenly Father gives us His Holy Spirit, so that by His grace we believe His holy Word and lead a godly life, here in time, and hereafter in eternity.

THE THIRD PETITION.

Thy will be done on earth, as it is in heaven.

What does this mean? Answer:

The good and gracious will of God is done indeed without our prayer; but we pray in this petition that it may be done among us also.

How is this done? Answer:

When God breaks and hinders every evil counsel and will which would not let us hallow God's name nor let His kingdom come, such as the will of the devil, the world, and our flesh; but strengthens and preserves us steadfast in His Word and faith unto our end. This is His gracious and good will.

THE FOURTH PETITION.

Give us this day our daily bread.

What does this mean? Answer:

God gives daily bread indeed without our prayer, also to all the wicked; but we pray in this petition that He would lead us to know it, and to receive our daily bread with thanksgiving.

What, then, is meant by daily bread? Answer:

Everything that belongs to the support and wants of the body, such as food, drink, clothing, shoes, house, home, field, cattle, money, goods, a pious spouse, pious children, pious servants, pious and faithful rulers, good government, good weather, peace, health, discipline, honor, good friends, faithful neighbors, and the like.

THE FIFTH PETITION.

And forgive us our trespasses, as we forgive those who trespass against us.

What does this mean? Answer:

We pray in this petition that our Father in heaven would not look upon our sins, nor on their account deny our prayer; for we are worthy of none of the things for which we pray, neither have we deserved them; but that He would grant them all to us by grace; for we daily sin much and indeed deserve nothing but punishment: so will we also heartily forgive and readily do good to those who sin against us.

THE SIXTH PETITION.

And lead us not into temptation.

What does this mean? Answer:

God indeed tempts no one; but we pray in this petition that God would guard and keep us, so that the devil, the world, and our flesh may not deceive us, nor seduce us into misbelief, despair, and other great shame and vice; and though we be assailed by them, that still we may finally overcome, and obtain the victory.

THE SEVENTH PETITION.

But deliver us from evil.

What does this mean? Answer:

We pray in this petition, as the sum of all, that our Father in heaven would deliver us from every evil of body and soul, property and honor, and finally, when our last hour has come, grant us a blessed end, and graciously take us from this vale of tears to Himself in heaven.

Amen.

What does this mean? Answer:

That I should be certain that these petitions are acceptable to our Father in heaven and heard; for He Himself has commanded us so to pray, and has promised to hear us. Amen, Amen, that is, yea, yea, it shall be so.

The Sacrament of Holy Baptism,
AS THE HEAD OF THE FAMILY SHOULD TEACH IT
IN ALL SIMPLICITY TO HIS HOUSEHOLD.

FIRST.

What is Baptism? Answer:

Baptism is not simple water only, but it is the water comprehended in God's command and connected with God's word.

Which is that word of God? Answer:

Christ, our Lord, says in the last chapter of Matthew: Go ye and teach all nations, baptizing them in the name of the Father, and of the Son, and of the Holy Ghost.

SECONDLY.

What does Baptism give or profit? Answer:

It works forgiveness of sins, delivers from death and the devil, and gives eternal salvation to all who believe this, as the words and promises of God declare.

Which are such words and promises of God? Answer:

Christ, our Lord, says in the last chapter of Mark: He that believeth and is baptized, shall be saved; but he that believeth not, shall be damned.

THIRDLY.

How can water do such great things? Answer:

It is not the water indeed that does them, but the word of God which is in and with the water, and faith which trusts such word of God in the water. For without the word of God the water is simple water, and no baptism. But with the word of God it is a baptism, that is, a gracious water of life and a washing of regeneration in the Holy Ghost, as St. Paul says, Titus, chapter third: By the washing of regeneration, and renewing of the Holy Ghost, which He shed on us abundantly through Jesus Christ, our Savior; that being justified by His grace, we should be made heirs according to the hope of eternal life. This is a faithful saying.

FOURTHLY.

What does such baptizing with water signify? Answer:

It signifies that the old Adam in us should, by daily contrition and repentance, be drowned and die with all sins and evil lusts and, again, a new man daily come forth and arise, who shall live before God in righteousness and purity forever.

Where is this written? Answer:

St. Paul says, Romans, chapter sixth: We are buried with Christ by baptism into death; that like as He was raised up from the dead by the glory of the Father, even so we also should walk in newness of life.

The Office of the Keys,

As the head of the family should teach it in all simplicity to his household.

What is the office of the keys? Answer:

It is the peculiar church power which Christ has given to His Church on earth to forgive the sins of penitent sinners unto them, but to retain the sins of the impenitent, as long as they do not repent.

Where is this written? Answer:

Thus writes the holy Evangelist John, chapter twentieth: The Lord Jesus breathed on His disciples, and saith unto them, Receive ye the Holy Ghost: whosesoever sins ye remit, they are remitted unto them; and whoseover sins ye retain, they are retained.

What do you believe according to these words? Answer:

I believe that when the called ministers of Christ deal with us by His divine command, especially when they exclude manifest and impenitent sinners from the Christian congregation, and, again, when they absolve those who repent of their sins and are willing to amend, this is as valid and certain, in heaven also, as if Christ, our dear Lord, dealt with us Himself.

How the unlearned should be taught to confess.

What is confession? Answer:

Confession embraces two parts: one is that we confess our sins; the other, that we receive absolution or forgiveness from the confessor,* as from God Himself, and in no wise doubt, but firmly believe, that by it our sins are forgiven before God in heaven.

What sins should we confess? Answer:

Before God we should plead guilty of all sins, even of those which we do not know, as we do in the Lord's Prayer; but before the confessor we should confess those sins only which we know and feel in our hearts.

Which are these? Answer:

Here consider your station according to the Ten Commandments, whether you are a father, mother, son, daughter, master, mistress, servant; whether you have been disobedient, unfaithful, slothful; whether you have grieved any peron by word or deed; whether you have stolen, neglected or wasted aught, or done other injury.

Pray, give me a brief form of confession. Answer:

Say to the confessor, Reverend and dear Sir, I beseech you to hear my confession, and pronounce forgiveness to me, for God's sake.

Proceed!

I, a poor sinner, confess myself before God guilty of all sins. Especially do I confess before you that I am a servant, etc., but, alas! I serve my master unfaithfully; for in this and in that I have not done what they commanded me; I have provoked them to anger and profane words, have been negligent and have not prevented injury, have been immodest in words and deeds, have quarreled with my equals, have murmured and used profane words against my mistress, etc. For all this I am sorry, and implore grace; I promise amendment.

*or pastor.

A master, or mistress may say:

Especially do I confess before you that I have not faithfully trained my children and household to the glory of God; I have used profane language, set a bad example by indecent words and deeds, have done my neighbor harm and spoken evil of him, have overcharged and given false ware and short measure;—

and whatever else he has done against God's Commandments and his station, etc.

But if any one does not find himself burdened with such or greater sins, he should not trouble himself on that account, nor seek or invent other sins, and thus make confession a torture; but simply mention one or two that you know, after this manner: Especially do I confess that I have once been profane; I have once used improper words; I have once neglected this or that, etc. Let that suffice.

But if you are conscious of none at all, which, however, is scarcely possible, then mention none at all in particular, but receive absolution upon the general confession which you make before God to the confessor.

Then shall the confessor say:

God be merciful to thee, and strengthen thy faith. Amen.

Furthermore:

Dost thou belive that my forgiveness is God's forgiveness?

Answer:

Yes, I believe.

Then he shall say:

Be it unto thee as thou believest. And I, by the command of our Lord Jesus Christ, forgive thee thy sins, in the name of the Father, and of the Son, and of the Holy Ghost. Amen.
Depart in peace.

Those, however, whose conscience is heavily burdened, or who are troubled and tempted, the confessor will know how to comfort and incite to faith with more passages of Scripture. This is designed merely to be a general form of confession for the unlearned.

The Sacrament of the Altar,
AS THE HEAD OF THE FAMILY SHOULD TEACH IT IN ALL SIMPLICITY TO HIS HOUSEHOLD.

What is the Sacrament of the Altar? Answer:

It is the true body and blood of our Lord Jesus Christ, under the bread and wine for us Christians to eat and to drink, instituted by Christ Himself.

Where is this written? Answer:

The holy Evangelists, Matthew Mark, Luke, and St. Paul, write thus:

Our Lord Jesus Christ, the same night in which He was betrayed, took bread; and when He had given thanks, He brake it, and gave it to His disciples, and said, Take, eat; this is my body, which is given for you: this do, in remembrance of me. After the same manner also He took the cup, when He had supped, gave thanks, and gave it to them, saying, Take, drink ye all of it; this cup is the new testament in my blood, which is shed for you for the remission of sins: this do ye, as oft as ye drink it, in remembrance of me.

What is the benefit of such eating and drinking? Answer:

That is shown us by these words, "Given, and shed for you for the remission of sins;" namely, that in the Sacrament forgiveness of sin, life, and salvation are given us through these words. For where there is forgiveness of sin, there is also life and salvation.

How can bodily eating and drinking do such great things?
Answer:

It is not the eating and drinking, indeed, that does them, but the words here written, "Given, and shed for you for the remission of sins;" which words, beside the bodily eating and drinking, are as the chief thing in the Sacrament; and he that believes these words, has what they say and express, namely, the forgiveness of sins.

Who, then, receives such Sacrament worthily? Answer:

Fasting and bodily preparation is, indeed, a fine outward training; but he is truly worthy and well prepared who has faith in these words, "Given, and shed for you for the remission of sins." But he that does not believe these words, or doubts, is unworthy and unprepared; for the words, "For you," require all hearts to believe.

How The Head of the Family
SHOULD TEACH HIS HOUSEHOLD TO PRAY MORNING AND EVENING.

MORNING PRAYER.

In the morning, when you get up, make the sign of the holy cross, and say:

In the name of God the Father, Son, and Holy Ghost. Amen.

Then, kneeling or standing, repeat the Creed and the Lord's Prayer. If you choose, you may also say this little prayer:

I thank Thee, my Heavenly Father, through Jesus Christ, Thy dear Son, that Thou hast kept me this night from all harm and danger; and I pray Thee that Thou wouldst keep me this day also from sin and every evil, that all my doings and life may please Thee. For into Thy hands I commend myself, my body and soul, and all things. Let Thy holy angel be with me, that the wicked foe may have no power over me. Amen.

Then go joyfully to your work, singing a hymn, like that on the Ten Commandments, or whatever your devotion may suggest.

EVENING PRAYER

In the evening, when you go to bed, make the sign of the holy cross, and say:

In the name of God the Father, Son, and Holy Ghost. Amen.

Then, kneeling or standing, repeat the Creed and the Lord's Prayer. If you choose, you may also say this little prayer:

I thank Thee, my Heavenly Father, through Jesus Christ, Thy dear Son, that Thou hast graciously kept me this day; and I pray Thee that Thou wouldst forgive me all my sins where I have done wrong, and graciously keep me this night. For into Thy hands I commend myself, my body and soul, and all things. Let

Thy holy angel be with me, that the wicked foe may have no power over me. Amen.

Then go to sleep at once and in good cheer.

How The Head of the Family
SHOULD TEACH HIS HOUSEHOLD TO ASK A BLESSING AND RETURN THANKS.

The children and servants shall go to the table reverently, fold their hands, and say:

The eyes of all wait upon Thee, O Lord, and Thou givest them their meat in due season; Thou openest Thy hands and satisfiest the desire of every living thing.

Then shall be said the Lord's Prayer, and the following:

Lord God, Heavenly Father, bless us and these Thy gifts which we receive from Thy bountiful goodness, through Jesus Christ, our Lord. Amen.

THANKS.

Also, after eating they shall, in like manner, reverently and with folded hands say:

O give thanks unto the Lord, for He is good; for His mercy endureth forever. He giveth food to all flesh: He giveth to the beast his food; and to the young ravens which cry. He delighteth not in the strength of the horse. He taketh not pleasure in the legs of a man. The Lord taketh pleasure in them that fear Him, in those that hope in His mercy.

Then shall be said the Lord's Prayer, and the following:

We thank Thee, Lord God, Heavenly Father, through Jesus Christ, our Lord, for all Thy benefits, who livest and reignest for ever and ever. Amen.

Table of Duties;

OR, CERTAIN PASSAGES OF SCRIPTURE FOR VARIOUS HOLY
ORDERS AND ESTATES, WHEREBY THESE ARE SEVERALLY TO
BE ADMONISHED OF THEIR OFFICE AND DUTY.

To Bishops, Pastors, and Preachers.

A bishop must be blameless, the husband of one wife, vigilant,
sober, of good behavior, given to hospitality, apt to teach; not
given to wine, no striker, not greedy of filthy lucre; but patient,
not a brawler, not covetous; one that ruleth well his own house,
having his children in subjection with all gravity; not a novice.
Holding fast the faithful Word as he hath been taught, that he
may be able by sound doctrine both to exhort and to convince
the gainsayers. 1 Tim. 3, 2. 3. 4. 6. Tit. 1, 9.

What the Hearers Owe to Their Pastors.

Eat and drink such things as they give: for the laborer is worthy
of his hire. Luke 10, 7.
Even so hath the Lord ordained, that they which preach the
Gospel should live of the Gospel. 1 Cor. 9, 14.
Let him that is taught in the Word communicate unto him that
teacheth in all good things. Be not deceived; God is not mocked;
for whatsoever a man soweth, that shall he also reap. Gal. 6, 6.
7.
Let the elders that rule well be counted worthy of double honor,
especially they who labor in the Word and doctrine. For the
Scripture saith, Thou shalt not muzzle the ox that treadeth out
the corn; and the laborer is worthy of his reward. 1 Tim. 5, 17.
18.
And we beseech you, brethren, to know them which labor
among you, and are over you in the Lord and admonish you;
and to esteem them very highly in love for their work's sake.
And be at peace among yourselves. 1 Thess. 5, 12. 13.
Obey them that have the rule over you, and submit yourselves;
for they watch for your souls, as they that must give account,

that they may do it with joy, and not with grief; for that is unprofitable for you. Hebr. 13, 17.

OF CIVIL GOVERNMENT.

Let every soul be subject unto the higher powers. For there is no power but of God: the powers that be are ordained of God. Whosoever therefore resisteth the power, resisteth the ordinance of God: and they that resist shall receive to themselves damnation. For rulers are not a terror to good works, but to the evil. Wilt thou then not be afraid of the power? do that which is good, and thou shalt have praise of the same: for he is the minister of God to thee for good. But if thou do that which is evil, be afraid; for he beareth not the sword in vain: for he is the minister of God, a revenger to execute wrath upon him that doeth evil. Rom. 13, 1—4.

OF SUBJECTS.

Render unto Caesar the things which are Caesar's; and unto God the things that are God's. Matt. 22, 21.

Wherefore ye must needs be subject, not only for wrath, but also for conscience' sake. For, for this cause pay ye tribute also: for they are God's ministers, attending continually upon this very thing. Render therefore to all their dues: tribute, to whom tribute is due; custom, to whom custom; fear, to whom fear; honor, to whom honor. Rom. 13, 5—7.

I exhort therefore, that, first of all, supplications, prayers, intercessions, and giving of thanks be made for all men; for kings, and for all that are in authority; that we may lead a quiet and peaceable life in all godliness and honesty. For this is good and acceptable in the sight of God our Savior. 1 Tim. 2, 1—3.

Put them in mind to be subject to principalities and powers, to obey magistrates, to be ready to every good work. Tit. 3, 1.

Submit yourselves to every ordinance of man for the Lord's sake: whether it be to the king, as supreme; or unto governors, as unto them that are sent by him for the punishment of evildoers, and for the praise of them that do well. 1 Pet. 2, 13. 14.

To Husbands.

Likewise, ye husbands, dwell with them according to knowledge, giving honor unto the wife, as unto the weaker vessel, and as being heirs together of the grace of life; that your prayers be not hindered. And be not bitter against them. 1 Pet. 3, 7. Col. 3, 19.

To Wives.

Wives, submit yourselves unto your own husbands, as unto the Lord. Eph. 5, 22.

Even as Sarah obeyed Abraham, calling him lord; whose daughters ye are, as long as ye do well, and are not afraid with any amazement. 1 Pet. 3, 5. 6.

To Parents.

And, ye fathers, provoke not your children to wrath: but bring them up in the nurture and admonition of the Lord. Eph. 6, 4.

To Children.

Children, obey your parents in the Lord: for this is right. Honor thy father and mother; which is the first commandment with promise; that it may be well with thee, and thou mayest live long on the earth. Eph. 6, 1—3.

To Servants, Hired Men, and Laborers.

Servants, be obedient to them that are your masters according to the flesh, with fear and trembling, in singleness of your heart, as unto Christ; not with eye-service, as men-pleasers; but as the servants of Christ, doing the will of God from the heart; with good will doing service, as to the Lord, and not to men: knowing that whatsoever good thing any man doeth, the same shall he receive of the Lord, whether he be bond or free. Eph. 6, 5—8.

To Masters and Mistresses.

And, ye masters, do the same things unto them, forbearing threatening: knowing that your Master also is in heaven; neither is there respect of persons with Him. Eph. 6, 9.

To the Young in General.

Likewise, ye younger, submit yourselves unto the elder. Yea, all of you be subject one to another, and be clothed with humility: for God resisteth the proud, and giveth grace to the humble. Humble yourselves, therefore, under the mighty hand of God, that He may exalt you in due time. 1 Pet. 5, 5. 6.

To Widows.

Now she that is a widow indeed, and desolate, trusteth in God, and continueth in supplications and prayers night and day. But she that liveth in pleasure, is dead while she liveth. 1 Tim. 5, 5. 6.

To All in Common.

Thou shalt love thy neighbor as thyself. Herein are comprehended all the commandments. Rom. 13, 9. And persevere in prayer for all men. 1 Tim. 2, 1.

> Let each his lesson learn with care,
> And all the household well shall fare.

Christian Questions
With their answers,
drawn up by Dr. Martin Luther for those who intend to go to the sacrament.

After confession and instruction in the Ten Commandments, Creed, Lord's Prayer, and the sacraments of Baptism and the Holy Supper, the confessor may ask, or one may ask himself:—

1. Do you believe that you are a sinner? Answer:

Yes, I believe it; I am a sinner.

2. How do you know this? Answer:

From the Ten Commandments; these I have not kept.

3. Are you also sorry for your sins? Answer:

Yes, I am sorry that I have sinned against God.

4. What have you deserved of God by your sins? Answer:

His wrath and displeasure, temporal death and eternal damnation. Rom. 6, 21. 23.

5. Do you also hope to be saved? Answer:

Yes, such is my hope.

6. In whom, then, do you trust? Answer:

In my dear Lord Jesus Christ.

7. Who is Christ? Answer:

The Son of God, true God and man.

8. How many Gods are there? Answer:

Only one; but there are three persons, Father, Son, and Holy Ghost.

9. What, then, has Christ done for you that you trust in Him? Answer:

He died for me, and shed His blood for me on the cross for the forgiveness of sins.

10. Did the Father also die for you? Answer:

He did not; for the Father is God only, the Holy Ghost likewise; but the Son is true God and true man; He died for me and shed His blood for me.

11. How do you know this? Answer:

From the holy Gospel and from the words of the Sacrament, and by His body and blood given me as a pledge in the Sacrament.

12. How do those words read? Answer:

Our Lord Jesus Christ, the same night in which He was betrayed, took bread; and when He had given thanks, He brake it, and gave it unto His disciples, and said, Take, eat; this is my body, which is given for you: this do in remembrance of me. After the same manner also He took the cup, when He had supped, gave thanks, and gave it to them, saying, Take, drink ye all of it; this cup is the new testament in my blood, which is shed for you for the remission of sins; this do ye, as oft as ye drink it, in remembrance of me.

13. You believe, then, that the true body and blood of Christ are in the Sacrament? Answer:

Yes, I believe it.

14. What induces you to believe this? Answer:

The word of Christ, Take, eat, this is my body; Drink ye all of it, this is my blood.

15. What ought we to do when we eat His body and drink His blood, and thus receive the pledge? Answer:

We ought to show and remember His death and the shedding of His blood, as He taught us: This do, as oft as ye do it, in remembrance of me.

16. Why ought we to remember and show His death? Answer:

That we may learn to believe that no creature could make satisfaction for our sins, but Christ, true God and man; and that we may learn to look with terror at our sins and to regard them as great indeed, and to find joy and comfort in Him alone; and thus be saved through such faith.

17. What was it that moved Him to die and make satisfaction for your sins? Answer:

His great love to His Father, and to me and other sinners, as it is written in John 14. Rom. 5. Gal. 2. Eph. 5.

18. Finally, why do you wish to go to the Sacrament? Answer:

That I may learn to believe that Christ died for my sin out of great love, as before said; and that I may also learn of Him to love God and my neighbor.

19. What should admonish and incite a Christian to receive the Sacrament frequently? Answer:

In respect to God, both the command and the promise of Christ, the Lord, should move him, and in respect to himself, the trouble that lies heavy on him, on account of which such command, encouragement, and promise are given.

20. But what shall a person do, if he be not sensible of such trouble, and feel no hunger and thirst for the Sacrament? Answer:

To such a person no better advice can be given than that, in the first place, he put his hand into his bosom and feel whether he still have flesh and blood, and that he by all means believe what the Scriptures say of it, in Gal. 5 and Rom. 7.

Secondly, that he look around to see whether he is still in the world, and keep in mind that there will be no lack of sin and trouble, as the Scriptures say, in John 15 and 16. 1 John 2 and

5.

Thirdly, he will certainly have the devil also about him, who with his lying and murdering, day and night, will let him have no peace within or without, as the Scriptures picture him, in John 8 and 16. 1 Pet. 5. Eph. 6. 2 Tim. 2.